THE LIFE OF THE SOUL

By the Same Author

Stages of Consciousness:
Meditations on the Boundaries of the Soul
(Lindisfarne Press, 1984)

Becoming Aware of the Logos:
The Way of St. John the Evangelist
(Lindisfarne Press, 1985)

From Normal to Healthy:
Paths to the Liberation of Consciousness
(Lindisfarne Press, 1989)

THE LIFE OF THE SOUL

BETWEEN SUBCONSCIOUSNESS AND SUPRACONSCIOUSNESS

ELEMENTS OF A SPIRITUAL PSYCHOLOGY

GEORG KÜHLEWIND

TRANSLATED BY MICHAEL LIPSON

LINDISFARNE PRESS

Edited by André VandenBroeck

This book is a translation of *Das Leben der Seele zwischen Überbewußtsein und Unterbewußtsein, Elemente einer spirituellen Psychologie* by Georg Kühlewind, published by Verlag Freies Geistesleben.

© 1982 Verlag Freies Geistesleben GmbH, Stuttgart.

This edition © 1990 The Lindisfarne Press.

Published by Lindisfarne Press
R.R. 4 Box 94 A1
Hudson, NY 12534 U.S.A.

Design and Set by Will Compute, Inc.
RD #1, Box 39, Hamilton, NY 13346

All inquiries should be addressed to the publisher

ISBN 0-940-262-33-9

Printed in the United States of America

Table of Contents

CHAPTER ONE

Know Thyself

Epistemological Reflections

I.

Phenomena of the soul can of course also be observed in other people, but such observations are not immediate; rather, they depend on the psychological phenomena's *exterior forms of appearance*. The extent to which the soul's movements reach expression depends largely on the individual and his circumstances. Insofar as they do appear visibly or audibly in behavior or in facial expression, however, it is left to the observer to penetrate the appearance, to categorize it, to interpret it. To that effect, he can do no more than draw on representations, mental images, and experiences that derived from his own life, and on a conceptuality gained through the self-observation of such experiences and images of the mind. This leads to the question: Is psychological self-observation possible? Is there sufficient autonomy, sufficient distance on the part of the observer, as there is in the case of sense perception?

This question can also be put in another form: *Who*–what agency of consciousness–is capable of posing questions and making observations about consciousness itself? Strictly speaking, this has to be the first and perhaps the most important topic for psychology and indeed for every science that wants to understand itself–because it establishes the very possibility of such a science.

Everyday experience teaches us that it is possible to exclude a perception, or even all perceptions, despite open, receptive sense organs: not to see, despite open eyes, what is going on in front of us, or not to hear when we are being called. Important and fundamental as this experience could be for a doctrine of the senses, it interests us now from a different and more general standpoint. For this phenoenon, be it brought about involuntarily, through distraction, or willed through concentration on a particular thought, manifests but an extreme form of a general capacity pertaining to normal consciousness: the faculty to be attentive, to use *attention* selectively according to our will. On the other hand, this phenomenon shows that without conscious and willed attention, little or nothing reaches consciousness of all that the sense organs are able to transmit.

Conscious attention is always selective: we do not perceive *everything* we could perceive–if we did, we would never go a step further in life because of the countless perceptible details at every point in the perceptible world. Rather, through selective attention, we limit our perception to one specific segment. We ourselves, through our will, determine this selectivity; it is not fixed, as it is with animals. We can change it: first I look at a picture or landscape from the point of view of coloration, then I notice the gestures of the figures, then the total composition, and so forth.

The phenomenon of attention shows an *autonomy of the conscious subject* with regard to the countless impressions to which it is continually exposed. This autonomy extends from selectivity of perception to complete exclusion of impressions, during which the so-called stimuli, the physicochemical processes in the sense organ, in the circuitry of nerves, and evidently even in the brain, continue to proceed normally–what is there to stop them?

Through this autonomy, we face the perceptible world as *observers*. Apart from extreme cases, such as mortal danger, for instance, the perceptual world *effects* in consciousness solely what this consciousness qualitatively and quantitatively allows. Impressions exert no compulsion; they do not immediately carry over into action; thus, they are not immediate *causes* of conduct. Rather, the conscious principle–"I"–decides whether something is to occur, and what. This naturally does not apply to actions that take place routinely and by nervous reflex, though to some extent conscious exercise preceded such actions as well. Where a human being does not act out of knowledge and decision, he either behaves in an unhuman fashion, or he reacts with trained reactions that were once consciously chosen and learned.

These considerations are of manifold importance to psychology. They stand at the beginning of our study, to establish the possibility of a science of the soul.

If psychology is to be possible, then there must be *cognition*.

If psychology is to be possible, then there must be freedom in observation, in the cognition of psychological phenomena.

Autonomy does exist in cognizing the perceptual world. This is proved by the presence (not the content) of natural science, even if the appropriate consequences are rarely drawn from this fact. Is there a similar autonomy of the investigative consciousness in regard to the observation of soul phenomena?

Consciousness can distinguish among its qualitatively distinct components (thinking, feeling, willing, and their conglomerates) those elements that are more or less conscious, i.e. transparent for consciousness and controllable by it. The fact that consciousness *suffers* this diversity (it did not create it) and that the differences in clarity are there *for a specific conscious subject*–this is the reason psychological problems, and therefore psychology, exist at all. If everything that could be experienced in consciousness were as transparently clear to it as thinking, a science of the soul would be neither necessary nor possible.

When thinking appears in consciousness in its pure form, unmingled with feelings and will-impulses alien to it (thinking itself is always willed, and its evidence always felt), then it is transparent to itself and is at the same time *self-observation*. It always knows what it is thinking; act and content are one. If a second thinking were necessary to make thought-content conscious, then the content of the second thinking would have to be rethought anew in order to make it conscious in turn, and so on, indefinitely.

On the one hand, self-consciousness depends on the self-experiencing character of thinking; on the other, it hinges on the possibility of remaining conscious in thinking although excluding sense impressions and their memories.

A distinction exists between thinking becoming conscious of itself, and the becoming conscious of other contents of the soul. Perceptions always become conscious through thinking; thinking tells us what they are, even if adults generally do not notice the thinking process—and some philosophies are based on this lack of observation. It emerges all the more clearly when children learn to speak and to think: for the child, for whom most perceptions are new, no such new perceptions occur without visibly intense intuitive thinking. At every point, the child must "form" the appropriate new concepts. In adults, this can be observed during rare, new perceptions; for in the case of habitual perceptions, the conceptuality has already become imbedded in the senses. In other words, for the adult, seeing is imbued with a conceptualizing activity that does not enter his consciousness. Thus he can recognize objects by sight, so to speak, without being conscious of any rational activity. But when I say "I perceive my thoughts," this perception cannot be distinguished from the production of thoughts and does not occur with the help of something else, of a sense organ, for instance. Rather, thinking perceives itself in its very results.

Thinking and perceiving are realms of the soul's activity in which the subject is normally autonomous: it thinks and perceives at will. In thinking, the content as well is determined by choice; in perception, only the act itself is chosen, while the content is given by the environment and cannot be changed or transformed at will. In the phenomenon of attention and detachment, however, the autonomy of the subject during perception is manifest.

We can easily observe soul contents in relation to which the thinking subject possesses only a restricted autonomy, or none at all. Feelings, and will-impulses charged with feeling–passions–have an independence with regard to the subject, a self-sufficiency, against which the subject often struggles. In such a combat, the subject often either succumbs or becomes ill, which is another way of succumbing. *Feelings*, in contrast to thoughts, cannot be immediately summoned, and when they break forth into consciousness, they are in no way observable from a distance, as is possible in sense-perception. When feelings are observable, we are generally dealing with their corpse, a faint image of them. From this cooled-down form to the irresistible conquest of the subject, there extends a continuous scale of intensities to which observability and the observer's relative autonomy stand in inverse proportion. Passions, inclinations, and unseen-through impulses obtain their power from the feeling mingled in them along with the mind's images. This *independent* soul entity, *detached from the subject*, is readily encountered when we attempt an exercise of thought-concentration, for instance. Thinking of a man-made object and imagining it, one finds, after a short time, quite different representations in the mind and thought-fragments in one's consciousness. Now one is dealing with associations rather than with real thoughts. This distraction through associative images that always have emotional entanglements is the work of the independent part of the soul.

The above mentioned liberation from perceptive impressions can be experienced in two ways, depending on the activity in consciousness associated with these impressions. It can occur either through unwilled absence or distraction, while the light of consciousness dims; or it can result from concentration on a self-chosen theme, while the light of consciousness increases. In the first case, as can be seen in retrospect, the content of consciousness turns dreamy, dull, and appears in finished form without one's own doing. In the second case, the content is formed in clarity through current conscious activity.

Autonomy and clarity of consciousness are linked: they increase or decrease simultaneously and with them cognitive capacity and the communicability of conscious contents.

Dimmed clarity of thinking or perceiving is due to disturbances of the cognitive functions. With feeling, however we are dealing with a qualitatively different experience: instead of being subjects, we become objects turned over to feelings–their emergence eludes our will. Feelings that appear in this way are not *cognitive* elements of consciousness like thinking and perceiving; they do not communicate a "something," but only themselves, as if the eye, instead of seeing something, were to communicate to us its own sensations–itching, movement, pains. These feelings cannot be immediately remembered, as can thoughts or the mind's images and representations. This has to do with their mode of appearance, which overpowers the subject. Thoughts, perceptions and representations always become conscious, clearly conscious, as past; feelings, on the other hand, emerge as elements of presence, but are conscious in a dim, dreamlike fashion. We do not consciously experience thinking, perception, and representation as *processes*; rather, we awaken through them and through their products. To the extent that we live, as conditioned by our level of consciousness, in a world that is perceived, thought, and imaged by the mind, this can be recognized as a world of the past. With feeling, man lives in a dreamlike presentness, just as he dreamily experiences, without the sharpness of wakeful consciousness, unexpected events for which he has no behavioral routines. Closer observation reveals that actually we always construct the "present" afterwards, with representations, and that in experience we are never wide awake. "Presence of mind" really means a momentary intuitive waking in presentness, yielding a behavior that afterwards, often after much reflection, proves to be the best possible thing to have done. In feeling we are not separated from experience; we remain in the present and are therefore unable to observe, as we do in times of waking consciousness. This gives feelings their warmth, their liveliness, in contrast to thoughts, which have exchanged their life for a past-quality.

Feelings do not transmit direct cognitions; to an outside observer, they characterize the person in whom they appear, the person who experiences them. They are conditioned by a realm of the soul in which the person is not fully conscious, not autonomous. He is predisposed to specific feelings: this endowment is part of his psychological nature; it belongs to his past, like his physical organism. His feeling life, however, occupies an intermediate degree of consciousness, in between the waking consciousness of the mind's imagery and the sleep-consciousness in which he faces his organism. Man's fate can largely be founded on the feelings with which he is endowed. They belong to his most private aspect, to his own essence.

One's own private feelings move along a scale ranging from "this is good for me" to "that is bad for me." Our egoity has its center in these feelings. That is why they lack universality, i.e. validity for others, comprehensibility and communicability; all of this is proper only to thoughts.

Normally we have no knowledge of the *will* in pure form. It is always bound up with an image in the mind or with a conceptual motif, and often accompanied by feelings. The representations and feelings become conscious, as does the result of the act of will, the perceptible deed; the will itself does not. Initially, there is nothing to suggest that the will can be cognitive, like thinking. There is a hint of this as regards feeling, such as in the feeling caused by the experience of art or in the feeling that accompanies an intuition.

The life of the soul usually consists of a conglomeration of non-cognitive feelings and will-impulses of non-conscious or half-conscious origin, of psychological and mental habit-formations and thought-forms that weave through the whole of it. Mixed into this conglomeration is the occasional lightning-flash of new thinking. This partly serves the self-sentient mentality, the ego, but it is partly the still-untouched universal, autonomous element.

Within the soul, we can distinguish autonomous functions as well as those that reveal a self-contained independence vis-à-vis the autonomous part of the soul. Thinking is autonomous, and so is perceiving to the extent that it is penetrated by thinking. The feeling entity, on the other hand, is arbitrary and autocratic, as is everything it stimulates and influences: associations, preferences, passions and the like. Characteristically, the autonomous realm of the soul is form free and thus capable of taking on any form, while the arbitrary intrapsychic elements are always seen in prearranged forms: chains of association, forms of feeling, pathways of sensation with repetitive trajectories, etc. This is why the non-autonomous element is also non-cognitive. Thinking can think any thought; associations or compulsive ideas are not cognitive gestures at all.

It seems that autonomy is initially purchased at the price of presentness: thought-contents, by entering consciousness, are paralyzed, becoming elements of the past. Everything that touches on the conceptual world loses its life. As a result, this (mirrored) thinking, though autonomous, is not sufficiently powerful to master feelings, let alone to understand or deal autonomously with the even less conscious movements of the soul. For psychology, this state of affairs suggests a fundamental difficulty or a challenge. The psychologist faces another person's modes of feeling from the outside; however, since he only has command of mirrored thinking as autonomous mental function, he is forced to understand by means of rationality the non-rational element in the other's soul, and this despite the insight that the psychological entity causing the problem is never rationally intelligible. This gives rise to the peculiar rationality of analytic psychologies, which try to capture the hidden part of the soul by detective work, drawing *conclusions* from little clues in consciousness concerning the subconscious irrationality that lurks behind it. Only by achieving a different level of consciousness would the psychologist

be in a position really to obtain an adequate understanding of the world of feelings, for instance, in all
its liveliness and presentness. Of such goals or
methods, there is nothing to be found in the literature of psychology.

In the foregoing observations, we described the
paradoxical situation in which psychology and psy-
chologists find themselves. It is absolutely necessary
to strive for and practice a profound *introspection*, so
as to be able to build up adequate representations
and conceptualities in relation to those independent
phenomena of the soul that face autonomous consciousness in their own self-sufficient manner. The
psychologist would have to be able to meet feelings,
will-impulses of unclear origin, and soul phenomena
of non-autonomous sources, with the corresponding
conscious elements of understanding, just as he
meets the thoughts of another person with the capacity for thought, or the sense of thinking. These
elements of understanding, yet to be acquired,
should on the one hand achieve at least the degree of
clarity exhibited by thoughts; on the other hand,
however, they should correspond to the liveliness,
the warmth, the fluid, mutually interpenetrating and
vaguely contoured nature of feelings. This task cannot be accomplished through capacities normally at
our disposal, through autonomous, but dialectically
reasonable thinking. To put it simply: feelings, in
their essence, can be known only by feelings–but
these must be "seeing" feelings, they must really
feel, rather than simply feel themselves. Just as

thinking is a "speaking" in its very nature, so a "speaking" feeling–a feeling that tells me something–must be developed. Just as thinking, through its open immersion in the *element of language* (not in the words of a specific tongue) is a *universal process* that is then reflected in the particular, a process that is individualized and then dies out in the individual,–so feeling, likewise, would have to lift itself into an unfixed language whose fluidity is better suited to reality. Willing has a similar task. We will return to this evolutionary potential in the next chapter. Here we will try to sketch the nature of the evolution.

II.

The task suggested here for the psychologist is identical to an ancient goal whose formulation, "Know thyself," may initially appear less demanding. But the paradox in this maxim is not hard to discover. Who is to know whom? When I turn to myself cognitively, the cognizer and the one-to-be-cognized are identical: even the latter is *cognizing*; he exists in the act of cognition. The difficulty lies in realizing an awareness within cognizing itself, since habitual everyday consciousness always awakens *after* the cognitive act, as a consciousness of its result, e.g. of the already-thought. For today's adult, "Know thyself" means above all the task of experiencing oneself as a cognizer, in the act of cognition, not afterwards. In ancient times, this maxim could also refer to other goals. It is modern man's Apollonian task to progress from a past-consciousness to a bright present-consciousness. At one of its borders, everyday consciousness encounters the limits of its competence, beyond which the normal feeling life seems to begin. Behind this, there spreads a subconscious realm of impenetrable depth, province of a psychology that recognizes nothing outside this realm except everyday consciousness. Were the human soul really structured in this manner, the task of psychology would be hopeless. The question must be asked whether waking consciousness is not able to experience other limits as well. Such limit-

experiences then could occasion a modification of
this dichotomous image of the soul, and indicate an
access to higher cognitive powers such as could cope
with the subconscious realm.

Limit-experiences of this other type can be discovered if the challenge to "Know thyself" is met, or
at least attempted, with regard to cognitive
processes. If the attention is turned to such processes, and not to the soul's darkness with which it
cannot cope, then the observer achieves limit-experiences at the border of the bright hemisphere of consciousness as well. These point to a region still
brighter than everyday consciousness itself. It may
strike the investigator that everyday consciousness
can discover its own past-character.

Important conclusions can be drawn from this
fact. Is it at all possible that the past exists for an
absolute past-consciousness? In the same way, an
absolutely determined consciousness could never
discover the fact of its determination (it would always obey the determining element, never diverging
from it), a consciousness utterly filled by past could
neither perceive nor express its own character as
such. Past exists only for what is present. And
though the present element does not experience itself consciously, it is *above* everyday consciousness
and is the agency that contemplates its own past, its
continually produced contents. This agency must
therefore operate close to the level of everyday consciousness. The possibility of new ideas, intuitions,
and thoughts points to such a nearby presence.

Nothing new can come from what is past. The study of how children learn to speak and think points very clearly to this element as the source of intuition.

Another limit-experience is illuminated by introspection when the thinker seeks to determine how a thought is distinguished from a meaningless (but grammatically and syntactically correct) chain of words. The distinction lies solely in the logicality or evidentness of the thought. But rational thinking will never progress beyond ascertaining this quality. It is in principle incapable of describing, explaining or enumerating all the characteristics of what makes something *evident*. To do so, it would itself have to make use of evidence once again.

Thinking, of its own accord, follows what is evident, out of a feeling on the part of the thinker, a feeling that guides the thinking. It is not a self-sensing feeling, it "feels" the logicality. Logic is not a normative, but an *a posteriori* descriptive science: it describes how thinking works. If it were otherwise, if we had to learn logical thinking (by scientific study, for example), then we would have the problem of understanding that science or doctrine without possessing logic. The "how" of thinking–that there is a "how"–is still noticeable for thinking itself, but can no longer be explained. Whoever, through inner attention, discovers the intuitive essence–immediate understanding–as the fundamental element of the cognizing human being, will not fail to notice this element's kinship to evidence. Belonging to the same domain is the barely acknowl-

edged phenomenon that thinking, provided it is
thinking something *new*, is *always improvised*; we
do not know in advance what we are going to think,
otherwise we would already have thought it.

disclosure

The last-mentioned limit-experiences point
concretely to sources from which consciousness
draws its cognitive powers. Intuition and primal understanding stem from this realm. Before something
can be explained, there must exist the capacity to
understand the explanation. The source must therefore appear to everyday consciousness as a more
light-filled region, or, in a higher sense, a more
"speaking," word-like sphere that contains nothing
that has as yet been thought, and is nonetheless the
possibility of every thought. As such, it is character-
ized as a not-unstructured realm, but one defined by
no specific form, carrying with it the power and capacity for every form.

It is well-known that the Aristotelian categories cannot be explained, nor can they be somehow
"derived." They did not, for instance, arise by ab-
stracting from a multitude of observations; the very
ordering of these observations into coherent groups
presupposes an ordering principle, and this is itself
the category. The category "being" does not come
about by observation of many existent things; rather,
I recognize them as existent because the category of
"being" is known to me before it has a verbal expression. The categories are purely intuitive formations;
only in retrospect can they become "abstract," i.e.,
not experienced, giving up their life by entering into

everyday consciousness, formulated and overlaid with words. Philosophic–intuitive–temperaments can always reactivate and reanimate them; in such people they regain their life. As living idealities, as universal wordlike forms, they make up the scaffolding, the fundamental structure, of our thinking, of our world view.

As with categories, so it is with every new thought, every new idea, every new understanding, everything creative: they originate in the life of the present. The essential thing in picturing this source is to understand that it must lie nearer to the light, nearer to the wordlike than the everyday or scientific consciousness that issues from it. That the understanding cannot be explained by, derived from, or "understood" through non-understanding–this thought contradicts much of what counts as scientific today, although such science is itself contradictory in just this regard. At some point, we have to think clearly through the fact that word, the wordlike, cannot arise accidentally, without a "speaking" subject; nor can it be understood without such a subject. Insofar as the cognitive capacities of everyday consciousness stem from a "more understanding" element, normally attainable by consciousness only as a limit-experience, this element can be called the supraconscious. If the psychologist intends to probe and understand the mental region that, as a separate formation, borders on the autonomous area from below, then he must make use of the stronger, more penetrating cognitive energies of the supraconscious.

Through their liveliness and presence, these energies offer adequate means of recognizing and even healing the subconscious.

Through the discovery and recognition of the supraconscious, the observer of the human soul is now in a position to see its landscape differently than is customary in psychology. The image of the soul becomes tripartite: the *supraconscious*, the spiritual element that reaches into the soul, source of cognitive capacities; the *conscious*, essentially autonomous thinking, an individualized copy of the spiritual; the *subconscious*, the structures composed of mental habits, forms, and patterns of behavior that are independent of conscious control and whose existence and origin are not directly conscious. The supraconscious is form-free, and is cognitive for this very reason, the possibility of all forms; whereas the subconscious consists of forms that are, while fluid and changeable to some degree, still very tenacious and self-conservative. Since the middle, conscious region is a sphere of pastness, the psychologist can only appeal to supraconscious energies if he approaches the subconscious. Since the "contents" of the subconscious achieve at most a dreamlike consciousness, they are not "paralyzed" like those of the middle sphere. Here the image arises of the suprahuman, divine conqueror of the subconscious dragon-nature.

Accordingly, the task and precondition of psychological research must be to extend the researcher's faculties of consciousness in the direction of that which is normally supraconscious: with *these* abilities he could penetrate the area that lies below everyday consciousness. This task is equivalent to a spiritual schooling such as has been followed at every epoch in an appropriate way and described for modern man through the spiritual science of Rudolf Steiner: as a schooling of thought, feeling and will, and as the possible transformation of perception –which presupposes a heightening of the three soul-functions. The practical psychologist can hardly put off his activities until he has attained these sought-after capacities. Yet he will be aided considerably if he approaches the soul and the phenomena of the soul in a more adequate manner by forming new and appropriate concepts. The "appropriate" concepts are qualitatively different from those of normal, even of scientific consciousness: They must be live-lier, more fluid, more malleable, even more exten-sive, without losing their clarity. Their formation is possible through the adequate *understanding* of the results of research that arose through heightened cognitive ability and have been transmitted in con-ceptual form. Whoever comes in contact with re-ports of such research should guard against trying to understand them with ordinary, habitual conceptual schemas: this would lead, and has led in the past, to their being widely misunderstood. In the following chapters, we shall attempt to sketch the psychologi-cal and mental functions, as well as perception and its possible development. This sketch can also be

taken as an introduction to the formation of ex-
panded concepts.

CHAPTER TWO

Universal Processes in the Human Soul

I.

One of the conclusions of the last chapter could be stated as follows: "If we cognized everything completely, there would be no self-sentient soul life." It is not difficult to realize, however, that without such a life of mind and soul, neither would there be, initially, any possibility at all of cognition such as we possess it today. The world–whatever may be meant by that term–would in its processes seamlessly perpetuate itself in man; it would sound through him and transluminate him, without the sound or the light being arrested, without their having an effect on him. At mankind's current stage of evolution of consciousness, it is inevitable that if the universal light is to flash up as cognition, part of it must have some effect on the human organism. Every cognizing must contain a universal component that is stamped by and characteristic of what is to be cognized. Human cognition experiences these components partly as perception, partly as the ideal conceptual element we are accustomed to ascribe to thinking. It is also through thinking that we experience the purely ideal, ideality as such, in the form and to the degree allowed by our consciousness. Thinking and perceiving create effects in our finer and coarser organism, to the point of affecting the physicality itself. They are "paralyzed" by this process, reduced, held up. The contents of thought and perception appear as the past-images of a life of which we glimpse a vague notion in the process of cognition, but that we do not consciously experience.

Thinking as well as perceiving are universal processes taking place in man. The objection that there are immense differences of opinion among people in regard to thinking only proves what it seeks to refute. For it is only on a common ground that differences of opinion or discussions can come about. The fact that they do arise hinges on our freedom with regard to cognition–as does our experience that error exists. That errors can be discovered and understood–and they *are* errors only if we *recognize* them as such–shows the universality of cognition. Views that explain all knowledge to be subjective uphold a weak position. On the one hand, they have to find some laborious explanation as to why a perceptual image is approximately the same for all observers; on the other, representatives of such a view fail to notice that their expositions could not be understood if they were right, if thinking were indeed subjective.

As universal processes, thinking and perceiving could never err. They might be limited in scope, and not take in all reality at once, but what they do grasp could never be wrong. In fact, errors are mixed into the universal processes of thinking and perceiving through the independent, non-cognizing, private

region of the soul. Where thinking gives free rein to
a prejudice conditioned by feeling, there error arises.
Thinking can be suspended out of complacency, in
which case a pre-formed, ready-made element, unil-
lumined, comes to the fore without its being noticed
by thinking.

That universal processes are arrested in the
human soul and thus become conscious, thereby at
once losing their life and gaining appearance, albeit
reduced and paralyzed–this makes for the possibility
of *self-consciousness*. In the shadow caused by past-
consciousness when it separates the subject from the
force field of the universal processes, the human I
can waken and strengthen itself toward self-consciousness. From this paradox–that a *subject*, by
willing, lets *universal processes* play themselves out
in it–grows the human being, his suffering, his joy.

The private, non-cognizing, non-communicating, self-sentient region of the soul is built above all
from feeling and emotions that we know from everyday life. This emotional entity is non-cognizing and
non-communicating just *because* it is self-sentient.
And although it is self-sentient, the emotions always
grasp at something external; they cannot, like
thoughts, be called up at choice by the subject, and
they come and go independently of the will of the
person who suffers them.

Self-sentience is not immediate self-sentiency
on the part of the subject, nor is it self-perception:
rather, the subject suffers–and indeed wants to suffer–feelings that feel *themselves* as pleasure and also

as pain. For the subject, these feelings are perceptions by which it is swept along, and over which it
has almost as little power as over sense-perceptions.
The soul can draw back from the latter, but it is difficult, and often even impossible for it to free itself
from feelings. The separate, tyrannically independent part of the soul, as opposed to autonomous
thinking and perceiving, begins with the emotions.

Thinking experiences itself, and it is wakeful,
even though it experiences itself in its past; emotion
is self-sentient and dream-like, but it is *present*. This
is why the autonomous, thinking part of the soul is
practically helpless in the face of it. The subject
clings to self-sentience and experiences itself by self-
sentience, though this is, finally, a foreign element.
The thirst for self-sentience is the core of egotism.
The more specific egotistical feelings proceed from
this core, which is visible in the never-satisfied
demand for ever-new self-sentient–non-"speaking"
–feelings, and emotions that permit self-sentience.
Our yearning and desires do not want to be satisfied
once and for all. On the contrary, their essence is to
repeat themselves. They reassure the everyday subject as to its existence. The security obtained by this
kind of emotional self-touching needs to be continu-
ously corroborated. Such renewed self-confirmation
would be unnecessary for the subject if thinking self-
experience could occur not through the *already-
thought* but in *present thinking*. In that case, present
consciousness would be the agency within us equivalent to our emotions in intensity as well.

Summing up these considerations, we see self-sentience as a substitute or preliminary to a self-experience that is non-abstract because it is present. Self-experience concerns the I-being, while self-sentience concerns a soul-substance that we initially experience as dreamlike. If self-experience with a clarity superior to mental knowledge were possible in the present, the self-sentience of ourselves against the outer husk of ever-impenetrable emotions would be superfluous.

The question then can arise: would all feeling become superfluous? Would not the world be infinitely impoverished without feelings? What would become of that element we initially experience as feeling?

A thorough observation of the feeling-life cannot fail to notice that while a feeling arises as an inner experience, it nevertheless always requires an external stimulus, a fact, a representation, a thought. Generally there is no rational connection between this motif and the feeling. Why does an envious man suffer a gnawing feeling when someone else has had a success? And one's own lack of success can awaken a vexed feeling that has no sense nor purpose and hampers one's next attempt. The feeling has loosed itself from the gist of the circumstance, has become independent and tells us nothing concerning the circumstance. Yet it has preserved the unchangeability of a perception: once a feeling is there, it exists as unavoidably as does a perception. Although it is inner life, it has an independent life in the soul. This independent life of felt-feelings moves along the bi-polar scale from good-for-me to bad-for-me. The feelings, moreover, are not at all objective: something harmful can be felt as good-for-me–an error that never occurs in animals unless man has interfered in nature.

Self-sentient feelings can be contrasted with another, less well-known type of feeling. These feelings "say" something, even if what they say cannot be put into words. Such feelings are to be found in artistic activity, be it active or passive, in religious belief in the sense of Paul, Tertullian or Kierkegaard, and in the feeling of logicality or evidence. These feelings are not of a private kind; otherwise, artistic judgment would be *completely* subjective, belief would not be at all communal, and evidence would not signify a general validity. Feelings of this kind have an object outside the soul and refer to this object, not to the feeling subject. They are bound to an external object and they "say" something about *how* it is beautiful, *how* it is true, *how* it is logical.

These feelings are even more difficult to describe conceptually than the first kind; nor are they easy to observe. Although every normal person thinks logically, the supraconscious *how* of this activity is at best a limit-experience in consciousness. As such, however, the feeling of evidence along with the feeling of beauty and faith must be counted as part of the universal process that can appear in the human soul and that works its way into the soul through the feeling of evidence. These feelings, which are not self-sentient, really *feel*, as the eye sees.

In the light of these feelings, the normal self-sentient feelings seem twisted or spoiled. A similar phenomenon in the realm of thinking would be *association*. This is not thinking; it is not there for cognizing but for *itself*, in the guise of thinking, from which it borrows its external form. Wherever genuine new thinking is absent, the many downward stages of thought-like, ready-made "responses" to "stimuli". Everyday life consists largely of such stimulus-response behaviors as described by behavioral psychology. But these patterns represent precisely what is not specifically human in our behavior–the deadened portion of the soul that has turned into routine and habit. The *first* time, each stimulus had to be understood, each response had to be created.

The realm of reflex stretches from routine answers to pathologically compulsive ideas. Not only specific thought-formulas belong here, but whole characteristic thought channels as well, prearranged thought-sequences that often serve to avoid *new* thoughts. The outward form of this phenomenon shows thought growing wooden as it tries to master new situations and problems with old thought-schemas: mere thought-forms arise, instead of *thinking*. To be sure, a loosening of this crust often occurs in old age, and a great new sensitivity and receptivity for the new appear.

What we are familiar with as our habitual feeling-life is, all in all, analogous to this derivative, substitute thinking: like the latter, it is *formed*, even pre-formed. As if these feelings had fixed tracks to run on, they are never qualitatively *new*, and they move along the scale of their sole quality: "good-for-me" to "bad-for-me." And this is why, like the "response-thoughts," they are non-cognitive. It is easy to see that true thinking, which thinks new things, corresponds to *cognitive* rather than self-sentient feelings. Such cognitive feelings, as experienced in art, in faith, and in logicality, are the *original* feelings, and our accustomed, everyday feelings are separate offshoots of the feeling life that have become independent, just as "response-thoughts" are split off forms of the life of thought.

The analogy of the life of thought is also revealed in the monotony of normal feeling and in the unlimited, multicolored variety of cognitive feeling. The *already-thought* (response-thought) has been the occasion for attempting to formulate human thinking as a mechanism, or even to mechanize it, in accord with the assumption that its basic elements, which are conceptualities, are ultimately limited, i.e. that man creates no new concepts. This implicitly sets up the goal that there *should* be no new thinking or concepts; that thinking should stop and only its ersatz remain. An analogous dehumanization with regard to feelings is already far advanced, through ignorance of cognitive feelings and through the exclusive cultivation of self-sentient feelings. Psychology powerfully supports this in education and in everyday life, with its appeal to egotism as sole human motivation. The notion that man is "evil" or asocial by nature is based on observation of the everyday feeling of the adult and of the child whom this adult has spoiled. It is also based on the misinterpretation of the psychological life of children on the part of a psychology blinded by the dogma of man as essentially predictable and evil. It should be brought out that this dogma, in turn, has its precursor and origin in a decadent form of religious life determined by a guilty conscience.

The infant's feeling-life is largely *open*, i.e. not trapped in fixed, prearranged forms. It is therefore *cognitive*. This is most striking in the purely intuitive way the infant learns to speak and think: the understanding of words, of gestures, of the semantic and syntactic structures of the language, is made possible by cognitive feeling alone. Such "understanding" is not intellectual, of course. It is the best example of supraconscious understanding. Adults, too, speak at least their mother tongue almost perfectly, without knowing any of its grammar. Learning to speak is a kind of imitation, but it is an *understanding imitation*. Not just the acoustic phenomenon is "imitated" by the child, but the adult speaking to him, down to the source of the words, right down to the adult's thinking.

When and how self-sentient feelings arise in a child lies outside the scope of this study. Mentally and sensitively, the human child is not "locked in" to nature, to the world of perception, as animals generally are from birth. The activities of the child's feelings are largely free: after all, a child can learn any language from his environment, regardless of heredity. The life of feeling, is at least partly determined by this kind of "imitation" of the adult environment. But we must also assume that a component of this process is independent of the environment, deriving rather from the evolutionary fate of the individual, or of humanity: in order one day to become a free, autonomous individual, man must at first separate himself, in his feeling, from the "world." What the religions call original sin is the turn toward oneself, the backward-bend of feeling, from a state of sensing *that* to sensing *self*, like a radiant beam recurved into a self-enclosed formation. It is a temporary substitute and a preparation for the goal of becoming a self-experiencing light in the presence of the word. Instead of this, there arises self-sentient feeling in the dreamlike presence of emotion.

Living thinking, not as yet formed into words (it could be called primal thinking or primal understanding), is a universal process. Paralyzed by human consciousness, this universal process ends in the subject. Its *content* remains universal as long as it is not contaminated by non-thinking. As content, what has been thought can be formulated as a mechanism–and mechanized. Though "living," self-sentient feelings are altogether subjective, self-enclosed formations. They seem to be reactions, feeling-responses to stimuli or situations: a kind of mechanism. The open cognitive feeling-life, universal in character, is encountered in consciousness only as limit-experience.

The third function of the soul, the will, is known to contemporary man almost exclusively as a subjective element–if we can speak about its being noticed at all. What is usually referred to as the will becomes conscious as a phenomenon in the perceptual world, as the *result* of willing or as limit-experience of consciousness, as being-able-to-will or not-being-able-to-will. The subjective forms of the will always arise in combination with representations or conceptual motifs. There is no "empty" will, such that we could experience it without knowing *what* it wills. That *what* is an image of the mind, a representation, or a thought: these become conscious. In this domain as well, a hierarchy becomes apparent, a scale that runs downward from fully conscious acts of will based on knowledge and decision, through half-conscious actions grounded on a feeling, an emotion, or a wish, down to near-automatic, habitual activity doing out of habit, perhaps out of a habit of feeling. Though always determined by an image in the mind, the will presents itself separately from the conceptual realm: we can think or mentally picture something without willing it, or else we can realize that same representation through the will. If the will is set in motion by what is non-autonomous in the mind–against the true will of the I–then a situation that is fundamentally conflictual arises within the soul. Saint Paul was aware of this (Romans 7:15-23).

It is remarkable that the will never appears without representation in concepts or mental images, and generally to the accompaniment of feelings. This points to the original unity of the three psychical functions, which live separately in modern consciousness. It is not difficult to discover the unity of thinking and willing in pure, concentrated thinking. The more thinking becomes true thinking (the more it thinks something *new*), the more there must be a will there to produce this newness within thinking. In this case, thinking is an *illumined* will, very different from the "dark" will that is active in a bodily movement. Such a dark will is separate from the corresponding motif in thought–one need not actually carry out the movement one has thought of–but it never makes an appearance without a thought-motif.

In pure thinking, the will cannot be distinguished from thinking. It is not that one wants to think *something*–this something would then be already thought–but rather one is dealing with an improvisatory thinking-will. To the extent that thinking in its living phase is a universal process, the will is also identical with thinking. Thinking is alive just because the will lives within it. What rational or already-thought past-thinking lacks is the will; it has become cut off and can only be, linked to the motif as a "dark," a barely conscious mental act external to the motif to help the motif become realized. In pure thinking, the will lives at one with the feeling that guides thinking, in its supraconscious logicality, toward its goal of truth. In this *cognition*,

the three soul functions are really one, and they can
only be distinguished if observed from the standpoint of separateness.

Along with thinking, perceiving is also a soul
function in which we cognize. Although this capacity is closely tied to thinking, the role of will is different, at least apparently. It is *our* will that decides
what we think *about*. *What* we think is all the more
removed from our will as thinking becomes more intuitive and improvised. *Our* will must recede as
much as possible; the more purely thinking becomes
a universal process, the more it becomes a creative
thinking that thinks new thoughts.

In perceiving, when it occurs in full consciousness through selective attention, *our* will is used to
fend off distracting influences; *what* we perceive is
left to the universal will, which *speaks* out of the
environment of our sense organs. It is not easy for
contemporary man to regard what the world (especially nature) offers to our senses as a kind of speech
or writing–all the less easy because we do not understand the language of nature. This is revealed in the
essential difference between the way we see man-
made and natural objects. A man-made object is understood as such through its *function* as an object,
whereas no *real* conceptuality is available for natural
objects and natural phenomena. We do not know
their "function," since it does not correspond to the
notion of human purpose; we do not know their
meaning. We are familiar with the function of a
knife, and therefore with its essence. But as soon as

we consider what it is made of, we have a riddle: what is the function or meaning of iron, for example? A chemist knows little more about this than does the layman. And yet nature as a perceptual image is *language*, since it reveals qualities, lawfulness; it consists of this and that, of the specifically knowable. At first we designate natural phenomena nominalistically; but one can only name something nameable–something specifically conceptual, something wordlike. The nominalists failed to notice this precondition.

Nature consists of thinkability that, for the time being, we cannot think. Behind the appearances stands the will that brought forth this wordlike world. No word comes about by accident; there is always a will that speaks through it. It is, apparently, not a currently decisive will, but rather a set will; it does not change. If it were otherwise, no natural science would be possible. Just as the speaker's will speaks out of a human word or sentence, a will that is alien to us sounds through nature. We try to fit into this will in perceiving. We say: thy will be done.

The more our perceiving soul is stamped by the universal will that speaks in nature, the fuller our perception becomes. Conceptualities of a higher order are necessary really to understand nature, or at least concepts that are alive, as was suggested in the preceding chapter. How could we have a meaningful concepts of *life* if this concept itself is not alive? And so we have no concept of life–as can be seen from the scientific efforts to reduce the phenomenon of life to what is not alive and to grasp it by laws that stem from the realm of the unliving.

In thinking and feeling we find half-conscious and fixed forms alongside our more fully conscious activity, and we react to stimuli almost automatically with such forms. In the same way, alongside of conscious, *new* perception, there are more or less automatic, half-conscious kinds of perception. The latter are predominant in everyday life. Usually, we perceive superficially, with fixed representations. The predominant, deteriorated forms of psychological and mental life have largely determined the picture of man sketched by psychology, which helps to spread the diseased consciousness of our time.

In pure, intuitive thinking and in fully conscious perceiving, a universal will is active in man, whose direction is the *reverse* of normal willing: instead of going forth from man, it moves toward him. Even when man acts on his own, his will–of the same consciousness as dreamless sleep–is a universal power, which he has the use of because it has been separated from its suprahuman ideal or word-like part. This is why this will is not conscious as a process. The more the thinking that determines the will is intuitive, i.e. a universal process itself, the more the action will be *creative*, i.e. moral. It continues working creatively on the given world. And just as thinking and perceiving have their deteriorated, automatic, stimulus-conditioned forms, so too does human action, to the extent that it proceeds from half-conscious or subliminal impulses.

II.

In thinking, man initially brings a universal process to a halt: it becomes paralyzed by being reflected in the brain. But this makes it possible for man to take up this universal process and continue it on his own, through a new *beginning* in freedom. An analogous gesture is possible in willing. The difference between cognizing and acting is only a difference of degree–cognizing is not a copy, but a creation.

In thinking and perceiving, the universal word speaks to man, in man. All that can be understood by man–according to his evolutionary level–of the universal word, sounds in his thinking; in perceiving, there rings for him the wordlike that he does not yet understand, for which he has no adequate concepts. In cognition and in intuitive action the word, through man, adds something to existing creation: in cognition, ideas appear through man; in his actions, the perceptible world is altered. The *new* can only enter the world today through man, through his capacity to *set a beginning*.

Man realizes himself both in the cognitive life and in its higher form as intuitive action. The universal word sounds forth through him, through his setting a beginning. Since it is wordlike, it does not affect him *causally* or *compulsorily*; rather, man can understand it and then act accordingly–or not. He can take the word in hand; he brings it to a standstill, and through his *own* activity, can manage its continued sounding forth. And so human cognizing and action is at once "son of god" and "son of man."

But that is an ideal that is seldom realized. The course of the universal process, supraconscious for everyday consciousness, gets blocked in man. Self-enclosed, self-maintaining formations build up in mental, emotional, and volitional domains. Today, the life of the soul consists predominantly of the decayed, non-cognizing forms of feeling and willing, a conglomeration held together by the associated thought-forms. From time to time, *new* thinking flashes into this conglomerate; but this often serves the self-sentient soul and so it is not *pure* thinking. Still, if grasped by man, it remains in part the universal element by which he can work himself out of his sickness. Illnesses of mind and psyche are all based on the blockage of universal energies; and many physical illnesses are the result of long-standing psychological damage. Man's world-historical disease that culminates in the age of the intellect need not be a "sickness unto death": it is a necessary, but conquerable phase on the path along which man must now be his own guide–the path which leads him out from the creaturely realm and towards responsible continued creation in the world.

While it is a disease on the one hand, it presents a starting point for healing on the other–the healing of humanity. Thinking self-consciousness is capable of sensing its own boundaries, and of recognizing in such limit-experiences its next task. It can discover its own disease as well as the central symptom of that disease, which consists in a tendency, or even a mania, of tracing back to non-cognizing mechanisms the cognitive functions of consciousness. Such tracing-back would itself be a product of the presupposed non-cognizing mechanism which lacks all criteria for ascertaining its own truth or error. In other words: there would be *no one there* who could test the theory thus produced. It it not hard to realize that creativity cannot be traced back to its own products. For consciousness, there remains the task to turn itself to the sources of its creativity.

In order to promote such an effort, a complete description of a cognitive schooling would have to be given here. This would be a moral schooling as well, since cognition and action are closely related, especially on higher planes. That is not the task of this study; yet the general pace and style of such a path can be suggested.

The key to a schooling of consciousness appropriate to our time is the *attention* which we have come to recognize as the primary gesture of autonomy. During the schooling, attention is used and exercised in two ways. The two kinds of exercises are closely related. Attention is *exercised*, and that requires specially allotted time-intervals in the course of the day. The exercise is carried out in a concentrated fashion during these intervals; at all other times the practitioner lives spontaneously, normally. The less the mood and consciousness of the exercises are spread by normal consciousness over the rest of the day, the more that day will be transformed in the correct spirit as the effect of exercising.

One group of exercises has the goal of directing attention to limit-experiences in consciousness, to limit-experiences in thinking, feeling, willing, and perceiving. The other group of exercises promotes the concentration of thinking and perceiving, as of certain more complex expressions of the soul such as speaking with others.

At prearranged times, attention is turned toward limit-experiences in thinking. Through concrete thinking, i.e. through specific thoughts, the "place" and "condition" of thinking's non-specificity (from which all specificity derives) can be sought and touched on. Non-specificity is to be understood as a relative condition–relative to what is specifically thought. We try to trace the how, the logicality, the evidence of a sequence of thoughts; we try to *experience* the *unavoidability* of thinking; if, for instance, the value of thinking is denied, we notice that even this denial only occurs through the very same depreciated thinking. We pursue observations and thoughts about the nature of intuitions. We try to distinguish between intuitions and associations as well as to develop an attention capable of distinguishing the intermediate steps between these two.

In the domain of feeling, attention is turned to cognitive feelings, rare occurrences at first. They are to be found primarily in the experience of evidence and in artistic activity. The difficult distinction between a feeling for truth and a mere liking for something is very important here. One can attempt to direct the attention to the different *colors* of feeling evoked by different truths. The practitioner's observation of the cognitive element in feeling later grows into the possibility of strengthening this element. We compare the taste of cognitive feelings with the quality of self-sentient feelings. Through the attention directed to them, the onsets of cognitive feeling strengthen while simultaneously a new organ develops for this kind of feelings.

In experiencing normal feelings, one attempts, by way of exercise, to surrender to them completely, to let oneself be flooded by them. In the very act of *trying*, on the gently directive will, the experiencer is born, the *witness* of this inner wave that otherwise rolls by without real subject. The witness does not behold the wave with an intellectual, thinker's gaze, but tries to experience it *feelingly*, through a new feeling *within* emotion.

The investigating attention can notice the element of will in thinking, and can grasp the difference between this will and the will that is active in a voluntary bodily movement. The latter is always bound by a goal. To aid in the experience of free will there is the exercise of a completely purposeless, "superfluous" activity; for example, to walk in a circle every day at the same point in time, in the same direction. This should never be done mechanically;

one attempts to become aware of each constituent inner step; e.g. to distinguish between thinking about the action and the decision to carry it out; or even to make this distinction in thought, without carrying it out. During the action itself, consciousness should be fully awake and should test each detail as to intention and execution.

Perception is least accessible to inner observation. Nevertheless, some effort can lead to the experience of how we rapidly oscillate, during perception, between selfless surrender and withdrawal into self-experience. In this oscillation, the withdrawal leads to the experience of the self-produced conceptual element, while surrender delivers something that is not of normal, conceptual nature and that must be present if perception is to take place. One attempts to feel this latter component more and more through the attention directed toward it.

Such exercises already require a concentration of psychological capacities. Autonomous capacities can also be strengthened directly. Increased concentration in thinking begins with the "purposeless," hence selfless, thinking of a theme that is easily comprehensible and requires no new knowledge, no intellectual exertion. An appropriate theme would be a simple man-made object, whose essence consists in its function. One exercises concentrated thinking and imaging of this object in its external characteristics, qualities, and function, as far as possible avoiding all distractions. Later, one attempts to think the idea that lies in the invention of the object and that is identical with its function. The "thinking" of this idea is no ordinary thinking. When the idea arose in the inventor, it was both wordless and without any mental image. And this is how it is to be "thought" in the exercise. Wordless thinking *is* living thinking, and can, in a later phase on the path of exercise, be further developed into *meditation*. This proceeds from a theme that expresses an insight concerning the creative within man or in the world, and that can be only formally understood by intellectual thinking.

In perceptual concentration, we notice above all how strongly it is influenced by pre-existing representations; these images of the mind, because they are "superfluous," encroach on its precise execution. One attempts during the exercise to look or listen with precision, and to pay special attention to the perceptual objects' uniqueness, which cannot be rendered in thoughts or words. It is possible, however, to discover that these uniquenesses, despite their inexpressibility, are *wordlike* in a higher sense; they *speak*, like everything in nature: a suprahuman speech. Later, an understanding of this becomes the task of perceptual meditation.

In every era, it has been part of the path of schooling to gradually dissolve the habits of consciousness, since they hinder intuitive experience. For this, there are exercises such as described in Buddha's eightfold path, e.g. "right speech": When I speak, it should really be speech in the strict sense of the word–it should serve no other purpose than to address the other person and to communicate something to him. Generally, speaking occurs for other reasons; to pass the time, out of social convention, etc., and this is to be avoided during the period of the exercise. Content, kind, and style of speech should be chosen, regulated and supervised in strict consciousness during the exercise, and adapted to one's conversational partners.

Further exercises come about individually, to a large extent, out of the practitioner's experience with the earlier ones. They lead to a strengthening of the autonomous principle that is capable of beginning, the I-am, and to the extension of cognitive capacities. For a diseased soul (that is, more than "normally" diseased), they first lead toward health. Illness often indicates a heightened sensitivity for new kinds of cognition, to the extent, for instance, that the sickness came about through lack of cultivation of new, potential capacities. In such a case, rapid growth of cognitive powers appears after the return to health, or even before. With increased attention to inner equilibrium and balance, someone in this situation must guard himself against error and extreme views or behavior.

The exercises mentioned, or others like them, evidently can only be practiced by healthy people or by those who are only slightly ill. For the more seriously disturbed, the exercises can be modified appropriately by a doctor or friend–emphasized or altered in a form usable by the patient, but only if the helper knows from his own direct experience what the exercises are all about and what is the state of the person to be helped.

The way strengthened attention flows together with its "object" in each exercise, the way this object is formed or re-formed through this very attention, this is the first hint of an experience of what in former times, in India, was expressed through the sentence *Tat vam asi*–You are That. The disjunction I-World gradually ceases during the exercises, without the experiencer being lost. He realizes that "attention" in its new, strengthened form is a universal process whose flowing he brings about himself–and which is his own true essence.

CHAPTER THREE

The Subconscious

I.

The cognitive functions of the soul–thinking and perceiving–are universal processes at their origin, and to the extent to which feeling and willing are transformed into cognitive activities, they too belong to the universal Word as well. All cognitive processes work through the cooperation of man, of the subject who speaks and can be spoken to, who lives autonomously in the universal processes of cognition, and who initiates these processes through the capacity for *beginning*. It cannot be claimed of cognitive processes that they emerge either "from man" or "from the world." The man-world polarity does not as yet exist in the *process* of cognition: subject and object only become separate in the *result* of cognition. What is usually called "the world" is designated as such after cognition. *In cognizing*, the "world" still contains the subject; it is a monistic world out of which, through the paralyzation of ideas and representations, past consciousness arises, and with it the dualistic world view.

What is autocratic and arbitrary in the soul, and frequently works against the I's autonomy, begins as self-sentient emotional life. It has sealed itself off from the feeling that lives beyond form, to become closed patterns of feeling. As these relatively visible feeling-forms have cut themselves off, the further development of the emotions proceeds *downwards*, to where the gaze of everyday consciousness cannot follow.

At the beginning of the preceding chapter, we said, "If we cognized everything completely, there would be no self-sentient soul life." Now we can add: Neither would we have a subconscious, the deeper psychical strata that are related to the self-sentient entity of feelings. But we could also say: If we cognized *nothing at all*, formed no concepts, like a wild animal, then we would have no subconscious and no self-sentient soul life. Animals, aside from those that live with humans, are guided by a sensitivity related to their life-processes, and *this* sensitivity, this sense of life extends to everything in nature connected with their lives, even outside their bodies, far into the atmosphere, the weather, and even geological events, since their lives are embedded in all these processes. An animal has only "wise" instincts and drives. Wise instincts are to be found in man to a limited extent, and apart from these he often exhibits many "unwise" passions and instincts. In these, the self-sentient form of feelings and emotions is woven together with a volitional component over which the thinking subject has little or no power. Self-destructive or self-wounding will is unknown in the animal world.

The cause of all this is to be found in the fact that universal processes come to a standstill in man; he interrupts them. A part of these processes

becomes conscious for man; the remainder cannot
be grasped consciously because his consciousness is
not adequate to the task. This remainder becomes
"effect." It is not a physical, mechanical effect; rather, man is confronted by psycho-spiritual forces that
he cannot *consciously* receive. By the very fact that
part of the universal Word becomes conscious, these
forces are sealed off from the universal wisdom and
make independent "forms." Today, as subconscious
impulses, they erupt in consciousness, in human behavior. Self-sentient emotional formations arise out
of the cognitive forces of feeling that speak from the
world, forces that initially were cognitive, but have
not been consciously assimilated. This process can
be followed clearly with regard to the will.

What are called healthy instincts in animals, or
even in man–impulses based on the constitution of
the physical body or originating in life-processes–are
not only unseparated from their goal, from their motivation, they do not even differ from it. That is the
case with the desires of animals, and in part those of
man, e.g. with desires like hunger and thirst that are
not based on addiction to pleasure. The same could
not be said for human sexuality. What we call the
will appears in man alone. The mental image or representational motif, which has become detached
from the will, is the only part that becomes fully
conscious for him. This is why man has the use of a
will: Man can unite, with self-chosen motives or
with motives driven by his desires, what in natural
creatures is from the first joined to a "motive"

–though it merely appears as such by the fact of sep-
aration. In the human being, the unity of nature
splits into motive and will. The latter has the consciousness of sleep, but is available to be used by the
pure, autonomous life of thought–and of course it is
also available to the mental images that stem not
from the autonomous thinking life but from addiction to self-feeling. These mental images give rise to
the "unwise" instincts of man.

The formation of the *collective* unconscious is
closely connected with the possibility of human experiences at the limits of man's consciousness. As
has already been mentioned in the chapter "Know
Thyself," contemporary man is exposed to two kinds
of limit-experiences: to the supraconscious above
and the subconscious below. Because universal processes are interrupted by thinking human consciousness, the soul has limits; it feels itself as the consciousness of these limits. But the individual human
soul conceals a dynamic component: the Logos, that
"increases out of itself." It makes man into a word-
being, a knower. But it also means that man can
never be a finished being, complete in his development. He bears within himself the only living (that
is not subject to laws) germ in the cosmos, the
Logos. Up to the age of the consciousness-soul, the
pedagogy of humanity was able to work on this living entity in man. As soon as the human being–not
merely a few elect, but a majority of people–becomes
capable of looking at his own consciousness, at his
own past thinking, at that instant man's fate, his

consciousness, becomes his own responsibility. Everything "from outside" can only reach him through his self-conscious thinking–"I think, therefore I am." The Logos-germ grows in him continually; man extends his inner gaze to the boundaries of consciousness, up to the "threshold." The sources of consciousness are experienced as limit-experiences. A limit-experience consists in man having the experience: here is a reality; but *what* it is cannot be known by means of this consciousness from within its own boundaries. Now there arises either an *Ignorabimus* or the attempt to investigate the limit-experience without lifting thinking to a higher level. In the second case, there arise constructions like the "thing in itself" (*thing,* at any rate); the *unconscious* that is nonetheless thought and cognized; *matter* that has no qualities and yet is thought about; the "*stuff*" of all known substances. This kind of "investigation" will never be adequate to the reality that has been touched on, but for this very reason the "concepts" that have been built up in this way do not become paralyzed and command instead a magnetic emotional/willful power of attraction. They appear as subconscious collective inspirations and play a decisive role in contemporary human life. They live an inscrutable life, a life never consciously seized, and they drive thinking further along the accustomed tracks–always hostile to the Logos.

What these concepts have in common is that through them the attempt is made to think the unthinkable–that which is in principle unthinkable for consciousness *inside* its boundaries but is *felt outside* the boundaries. This results in the contradictory nature of these "un-concepts": matter as carrier of all qualities, but itself assumed to have none, is unthinkable and imperceptible–since only what has quality can be thought and perceived. Such non-concepts, which come from collective limit-experiences, form the real (and not C.G. Jung's) collective unconscious. They go unnoticed by a naïve-realistic psychology, hidden as they are by other supposedly collective elements, and in them this truly collective subconscious appears as a cognition, as explanatory principle, as scientific discovery: as the "idea" of a subconscious from which stems the consciousness that speaks about this subconscious.

Through confrontation with light-energies that appear at its limits, consciousness is faced with a choice: either it must push its limits further, i.e. raise its powers of illumination, lift its level, or the energies to which it is exposed will be led into the subconscious. From there they operate to "inspire" thinking as it rolls onward, unchanged; a kind of inspiration from which there generally arises the "dark"–unwordlike–mirror-image of the disdained light-energy.

In earlier epochs, the confrontation with ever-new spiritual forces occurred under the guidance of humanity's pedagogy: as the transition of culture, of spiritual life, into a new zodiacal constellation, to new gods, to a new cult as the sign of a change in the reigning gods in heaven. The light energies that surged around man from the spiritual and natural worlds (which were still *one* world) were assigned to gods; they were the gods' field of power; they were divine, personal, wordlike. Divine figures and myths were understood by initiates as images of the forces that had to be dealt with at that time. Out of them the powers of human consciousness were some day to develop. The images had an effect on the human soul when it "saw" them–when it realized them as spiritual gestures, gestures in cognition. They affected the soul in much the same way that a meditation, through man's initiative, today realizes itself in the soul. The plurality of the gods reflected the plurality of the existential realms of the world and of human life–aspects of life and of cognition. The gods were personalities with individual character, countenance and fate: man gradually learned from them to be an individual, an I. The divine figures were not contents of consciousness, but were rather the onset of specific capacities. It was possible to leave in their protection the realms guessed at beyond the limit-experiences–as long as an inadequate conceptuality had not been split off from these experiences through the activity of reason.

In religious experience, a heightening of consciousness occurs when the limit-experiences are confronted. If this does not occur, and consciousness works with the limit experience on the rational level, then the interpretation of the reality hidden behind the limit experience slips below this rational level. The so-called subconscious, as discovered by

analytic psychology, has several levels. It has a subjective, individual level, and a more collective one.
What Jungian psychology calls collective belongs altogether to the individual; the truly collective,
which is the insufficiently understood limit-experience, remains unnoticed by this psychology.

Just as consciousness is not to be pictured as a
vessel with or without contents, so the subconscious
is not a container or a "place." Everyday consciousness is always the consciousness of its "contents";
the subconscious always reveals itself as a concrete
effect on consciousness, in consciousness. It is
present for consciousness. To mentally picture it as
a place or vessel or power means that one's mental
representation is continuing to work on the model of
the familiar world.*

The *individual subconscious* was observed in
earlier times as an effective force directed against
the autonomously thinking and perceiving subject.
Today, these subconsciousnesses are mostly justified
and legitimized by psychology and anthropology,
and so generally raised to the rank of conscious
"rights" or "aims." This development only involves
a change in superficial thematics; it changes nothing
as to the fundamental structure of the picture: the
human being still does not *cognitively* grasp the feeling and willing elements in perception or thought,
nor is he able to think the idea element in natural
phenomena. The source of subconscious formations

---

* The so-called "empty " consciousness can arise at the change
of levels of consciousness.

therefore remains in existence. Modern man is no healthier mentally than in Freud's time; only the symptoms of the diseases have changed.

From the uncomprehended feeling and willing elements, non-cognizing formations of emotion and will are built under the aegis of egotism. These dreamlike formations, that man experiences as if they were a wave that sweeps him along, determine his life to a great extent. In comparison with concepts they are more fluid, less contoured; they flow into one another; they are conceptually incomprehensible in their essence, because they are alive, while conceptualities are lifeless. Out of these psychological formations, unless they are adequately cognized, there arise life-forms, life-habits, functional diseases and finally physical symptoms. If these forms go on undissolved–unilluminated by cognition–through incarnations, they can then be called forces of destiny. Psychological "forms," complexes, are comparable to the behavioral forms of individual animal species. They are not completely fixed; the reaction pattern of an animal can vary greatly according to the circumstances. Still, a duck always acts like a duck: its circle of interests is given, determined by its species. A "complex" is an inner animal form, a pattern of behavior or sensitivity that reacts to a series of stimuli.

In spiritual science, the totality of an individual's psychological and mental forms is seen through imaginative cognition, on the plane of presence or life, as the figure of the "lesser guardian of the threshold," called the *"Doppelgänger"* in its deeper layers. These figures only appear visibly to the human being when he has released himself, through conscious effort and evolution of consciousness, from his non-conscious identity with his "nature" as it has become built up in the course of his destiny. These figures correspond to the personal "sin" of which Paul speaks (Romans 7:19,20): "For the good that I would I do not; but the evil which I would not, that I do. Now if I do that I would not, it is no more I that do it, but sin that dwelleth in me."

The subjective subconscious, formed from the feeling- and willing-reality that has not been received according to its essence, shows great similarity among different people despite its personal origin. We can therefore speak about feelings in general, e.g. envy, jealousy, greed, etc. In this area, subjective and yet similar among many individuals, there belong those psychological and mental capacities, those powers of cognition and personality, that have not been internalized, powers that were presented to man in early times in mythology, divine figures, and symbols. If they have not attained their goal–Christian internalization in the form of "the Logos in me"–then they can emerge from the subconscious as symbols and figures–*as contents instead of capacities*–that seem pre-Christian, or would-be Christian, or even traditionally Christian. If they are neither memories of what has been seen or read, nor forms induced by the psychologist, then they are past-formations of the spirit that have now become psychical forms. They reveal themselves now in psychological and mental forms, as content, just because they have not been realized as capacities. These forms, archetypes, belong in every way to the same individual historical part of the subconscious as do the common, widespread feeling-types, from which they are distinguished by their degree of subconsciousness and by their pictorial form.

What can really be called the *collective subconscious* are the already-mentioned "ideas" deriving from limit-experiences–those attitudes of cognitive life, those collective symptoms of a diseased consciousness that go unrecognized by this consciousness. Experiences at the limits of consciousness are given to man today as tasks for independent development of consciousness. They are sites where the impulses of the *Zeitgeist*, henceforth to be cognized and realized by human effort alone, are revealed, as a challenge to take the next step. If this challenge is not understood or realized by man, then the limit-experience is changed into its subconscious mirror image. In this manner, representations, mental images, and "ideas" arise that have power over consciousness and thinking without being in any way logically thinkable: they are unthinkable, irrational, "inviolable" mental pictures, whose power stems precisely from the unthinkable feeling- and will-forces that were not consciously received by man in the situation of the limit-experience. Thus the non-concepts of quality-less matter and particles arise, along with the unconscious as fundamental principle, the many veiled forms of the statement "I do not exist," the thought pattern of "It's nothing but...," chance as principle of evolution, etc. Their common trait is that they all deny the word, the independent reality of the word. Thereby the idea of personality is lost; the world and man himself are conceived as the impersonal results of a series of improbable accidents–and meaning is ascribed only to the statement that this is so. It can be shown that the root of this train of thought lies in the loss of the idea of Logos.

The quality or conceptual content of our perceptual image–even if the qualities often cannot be formulated in words–its *being-thus*, depends largely on our cognitive capacity, on our consciousness. That the perceptual world *is there*, its existence, is a subconscious, compelling sensation that derives from an unaccomplished limit-experience of the incomprehensible in nature. We cannot think the function of natural phenomena with everyday consciousness, as we can for man-made objects, because it is a past-consciousness. What we cannot think–the more powerful ideality or wordlikeness –appears in perception as its "incomprehensible part," as the lasting universal ground, existing "precognitively" (in the usual sense) and designated as material, dark and idealess by normal consciousness, which is incapable of imagining anything more light-like. Its being mentally represented in *this* manner is a collective, subconscious "inspiration." The universal ground behind perceiving is the living

Light or Word, to be experienced in consciousness as living thinking; present, in process, timeless, in which being and cognizing are one. This is the Prima Materia, still without the forms and qualities of everyday consciousness, but as the possibility and epitome of these qualities, as their origin. "Matter" with no quality is the dark mirror-image of the Word-Light.

In thinking, we meet the same boundary of the supraconscious when we inquire about its guiding star: evidence. What lies behind limit-experiences is in fact unthinkable and imperceptible; not in principle, as is the case with the notion of matter, but only for that consciousness to which it reveals itself as a limit-experience. The cognitive light must increase for it to be perceived.

Through extension of boundaries, through elevation of the cognitive level, it would be possible for psychology to meet subconscious formations *appropriately*. In principle, it is well-known that this "irrational" realm cannot be controlled through rationality, since rationality, according to the theory, is a weak offspring of the all-powerful subconscious. Yet psychology has no other methods at hand. Even feelings are perceptions for which we have no corresponding, living concepts; they become "effects" precisely because we are not in a position to perceive them adequately. All psychological and mental forms are laden with inadequate conceptualities by a psychology that remains on the rational level. Only through such a process do they become the kind of structure we are familiar with: complexes, associations, archetypes, symbols, etc. They arise through the existing conceptual system out of a feeling- and willing-reality inaccessible to everyday consciousness: they crystallize around what is brought to them in the way of crystallization-seeds. This is why it is possible to "interpret" and treat one and the same image, symptom, fantasy, dream, in different ways. By imposition of "names," subconscious energy-forms are identified and become partially manageable. In treatment, a healing role is played above all by the conversation, the word, and by the human personality of the psychologist or doctor through the human relationship to him that develops. Real insight into the subconscious is only possible for a consciousness that has achieved, in the heights of supraconsciousness, a wakefulness corresponding to the depths and liveliness of the subconscious elements.

Increasingly, it is man's responsibility to guide his destiny by himself. His destiny consists in a coming to grips with the universal forces that affect him. The possibility of becoming conscious of them grows with time. If this possibility is not grasped, if man does not work toward the evolution of his consciousness, then the universal energies that have not been understood become subconscious psycho-spiritual forms, hostile to humanity. Their characteristic form will correspond to the individual's–and mankind's–failure to evolve in consciousness.

II.

In the age of the consciousness-soul, the human being once and for all loses the gods that could still be perceived "outside" in earlier times. Evolution offers him the possibility of discovering the divine in the life of his own consciousness–that is the essence of Christianity. On the other hand, he is now exposed, with no help from the gods, to feel-ing- and will-energies that stream toward him in per-ception and in thinking. Most of humanity is in no position to experience these forces as *cognitive forces.* This is why they become feeling-forms and forms of the individual subconscious–they become what psychology generally calls complexes, sources of non-rational behavior.

In the last two or three hundred years, man-kind has also been exposed to experiences at the boundary of consciousness, limit-experiences of his soul. This began in certain individuals as early as the end of the Middle Ages. These experiences meant a serious crisis for that part of humanity that had not participated in the evolution of Christianity–the ex-perience of the Logos-idea, the Logos-figure by which Christianity differs from other monotheistic religions–and for those who had lost the Logos-idea or God the Son since around the fourth century. And so humanity cannot experience cognition, the word-like, as a fundamental reality, and does not see in limit-experiences of consciousness the possibility and challenge: to form and understand the wordlike at the next-higher stage–living concepts, sentient concepts. It does not see in limit-experiences the approach of the very source of its rational consciousness, but experiences them as absolute, unpassable existential limits. Consciousness thinks about limit-experiences without changing its level–by no means a rational act–and so it becomes the victim of subconscious inspirations that arise when an intelligence hostile to the Logos takes hold of the still unmastered cognitive forces. It is these inspirations that can justifiably be called *collective*; for Western humanity is edging collectively toward the threshold of the supraconscious, or the spiritual world, without noticing it.

What analytic psychology does notice is the individual subconscious; part of it is then called collective. On the other hand, there exists a completely different realm of psychology, that of "cognitive abilities." This psychology attempts to describe cognitive faculties, their development, their sources, by approaching them, in the rational manner of natural science, from the outside–without noticing that this procedure is itself already a result of this development and its sources. This makes the task at hand unsolvable by definition; for at the start of the development of cognitive capacities there stands the child's learning to speak and think–a well-known riddle in cognitive psychology. This process, intuitive through and through, occurs purely in the *supraconscious*, without a trace of it appearing on

the plane of rationality. No child can say *how* it
speaks; no adult can say *how* he thinks. The rules of
speech are only grasped *empirically*, even though
everybody uses them "non-empirically," that is,
supraconsciously. And though the whole of modern
scientific procedure is built on this supraconscious
basis, it is unaware of the reality of the supraconscious. The idea of the spirit is at most used as a
synonym for cognitive capacities, but independent
reality is acknowledged for neither one nor the
other. For this kind of scientism, therefore, cognition and religion are "spiritual" (i.e., private and subjective) areas, to which, at the very most, Jung's collective unconscious adds a universalizing trait. The
creativity of human beings, rediscovered from time
to time, is relegated to this private area, and it goes
unrecognized that cognition, communication,
conversation–in art as well–would all be impossible
if creativity were really subjective and not universal,
or "intersubjective" as it's called today.

The origin of the subconscious, even of the collective kind, lies in the supraconscious. The two
realms are of the same substance: but the substance
consists of *forms* in the subconscious, while in the
supraconscious, it is to be found as the *capacity* and
possibility of taking any form according to the object
of cognition. Form and formlessness are relative.
What appears as formless or undetermined to rational consciousness, is form for the next level of
consciousness–*a moving form*, to be sure, not static
form. For example, the word "although" is devoid of

content for everyday consciousness, while for living thinking it is the concrete form of its own movement.

Subconscious contents are generally formed in two ways. Initially they appear as behavioral forms that can take on very varied appearances as seen on the surface yet represent *one* form in each case. They can also be formed through the concepts ascribed to them by "science," by the doctor, or by the subject himself: a second-order process of crystallization is introduced.

The image of the subconscious in analytic psychology is determined by characteristic traits of this psychology unknown to itself: by its naive realism and its psychological Darwinism. The latter consists in seeking the origin of the subconscious in a biological direction, in the body, and imagining consciousness as arising from the subconscious. Human freedom cannot be founded on such a theory, and its existence is denied—although psychotherapy tacitly presupposes such freedom.

Naive realism is revealed in that the psychologist and his science remain on the level of everyday consciousness, in therapy and in research, even though it is maintained throughout that this consciousness is incapable of glimpsing or affecting the subconscious—partly because the subconscious is imagined to be much more powerful than rational consciousness.

Everyday consciousness is a consciousness of the past, insofar as it becomes conscious of the already-thought, the already-perceived, the already-represented. Belonging as it does to the past, all this would have no further influence on the soul, were it not a mere part of reality, whose larger half–in terms of feeling and will–is not encountered with full consciousness by the human being. What remains unexperienced in full waking consciousness continues as an effective force, in feeling- and willing-forms that live on, half-consciously or subconsciously, in the human being. They form a past that influences man to a great extent: partly in dream-consciousness, partly subconsciously, it reaches from what came earlier in time into the temporal present and acts as a predetermined, selective pattern for new experiences. What is fully conscious for man becomes the force-free area of his freedom because it is a past-element in which he himself can make new beginnings. But beneath this consciousness there lies the force field of one's own past, a past that has not been similarly paralyzed through being mirrored on the physical apparatus. What erupts into consciousness from this realm encroaches on man's freedom: it is the only thing that can encroach on it.

The formative forces from the domain of the soul's past are alive and cannot be dissolved intellectually. They can however be met emotionally–as generally happens in therapeutic treatment–in which case new non-cognizing feelings meet the older preformed and preforming emotional configurations and impulses. The landscape changes on the surface, and that is often curative and desirable. A fundamental change would involve the dissolution

of the past forms through appropriately heightened
forces of consciousness. Psychology remains sealed
off from this possibility until it recognizes the
reality of the supraconscious: namely, that the
limitations of our cognitive capacities are closely related to the realm below that of waking consciousness. This recognition would transform the dualistic
image of the soul–consciousness and subconsciousness–into a tripartite image: the supraconscious, the
spiritual, would come into view.

In *consciousness*, there occurs a continual
formation and *dissolution* of what has been formed.
By cognizing conceptually, we make forms from out
of the supraconscious; when we "read," in a wider
sense, we dissolve what has been formed to let it
flow into form once more. The *supraconscious* contains the *possibility of all forms*, qualities and conceptualities that can arise in mirrored consciousness, and it also contains the formative principles,
the regulative element in thinking that consciousness can experience initially as the limit-experience
of evidence. For consciousness, the supraconscious
is formless, a "nothing," since this is a past-consciousness and so it can only conceive of static
forms and circumstances, while it has to borrow
from the supraconscious (which is all movement) to
account even for its own motion. (Zeno's paradoxes
oscillate between these two levels of consciousness,
between continuum and discontinuum, and later develop into the infinitesimal calculus.)

The individual subconscious is revealed in associations, forms of reactivity, mental habits, "sensitivities." What is the difference between an association and an intuition? An *intuition* can be followed, *retro-spectively*, by pure logic, and its meaning is understandable for anyone who can grasp the thought involved; an *association* cannot be built up logically and has meaning for the subject alone. The collective subconscious portrays the collective limit-experience in a negative way. For example, the formlessness of the supraconscious becomes the collective association of the concept of matter–a "concept" that is unthinkable, impossible to represent, devoid of all experience: no one has ever encountered this "matter", no one has investigated it. And yet it has "inspired" science and the consciousness of the average man for centuries. It has power, and power of a collective kind.

And how can we distinguish between a collective *association* of this kind and an *intuition*? Since it is collective, it has significance for almost everyone, much more so than an intuition, which can scarcely be reached without spiritual effort. On the contrary, the idea of matter emerges as if by itself in our "sensibility," and is affirmed by the same force that brought it forth. That this idea has been transformed recently in many ways is insignificant from this viewpoint. Its essence remains the same: something is being talked about that is by definition *unwordlike*, that has only *existence* and no form, i.e. without any *word* in a higher sense. This "idea" is *not thinkable*, it leads to catastrophe at every level: to logical catastrophe in thinking; to psychological catastrophe in the feeling and willing individual; and it leads mankind into spiritual and material catastrophe. For if matter, and not the word, is the fundamental reality, then man cannot know himself in reality as soul and as spirit. If he does not become aware of his spiritual being, his Logos-essence, then he is not free and can solve neither his psychological, nor spiritual, nor material problems: as an unfree being he can solve nothing at all, he can do nothing; everything happens *to* him. This threatens his entire existence.

Obviously, far-reaching consequences derive from psychology's lack of awareness of the supraconscious, the spirit. The difference between association and intuition gets blurred. The confusion of above and below results, within the dualistic mental model, in a search for religious reality and roots within the subconscious, instead of finding them in the region and in the direction from which our cognitive forces come. As subconscious sources, however, these would necessarily have to be darker than the cognitive forces with which they are sought. Theology–"depth-theology"–having no religious experience to work from, welcomes this "help" from psychology: and so it can at least establish religion as necessary to mental health. Spirit–cognitive light–is as secondary for this way of looking at things as it is for naive empiricism. This psychology always deals with contents, never with the forces from which these contents stem. It concerns itself with the past-image of the soul, i.e., it always remains outside the soul. It could only shift to the inside if it were capable of perceiving its own present mental gestures, or if it were capable of investigating the life of another person's soul with imaginative consciousness. Psychology looks at what is easy to see, past mental phenomena, facts, complexes, archetypes, and not at the movement with which these appear, through which we perceive them. It is not the *effective* past that appears to this psychology, but that which the past has effected.

Forces of the past, continuing to work, keep the soul from realizing its presentness *now*. Stemming from the collective limit-experience, the collective subconscious inspiration of an unwordlike universal ground–matter, thing-in-itself, the subconscious –prevents the intuition of the Logos. This inspiration arose from the rejected intuition of the Logos, and the rejection *is* this inspiration (they are not related as cause and effect).

Once the unwordlike universal ground is assumed–sensorially assumed–then it becomes possible to trace back the cognitive functions of consciousness, in fact all functions of consciousness, to a mechanism, to the non-cognitive. But if cognition is determined, absolutely determined, then it is a natural process: neither proof nor refutation is possible, since there is no longer *anyone* there capable of doing these things. This is a second logical catastrophe. Since the unwordlike primal substance is not to be established through logical thinking, but appears in thinking consciousness as "justified" by an irrational feeling, this "idea" is practically impervious to logical considerations.

When the subconscious inspiration of the unwordlike takes root in thinking consciousness, it pervades the whole of human intellectual life and lends it a tone of impersonality and of partiality. The *responsible* subject is effaced, assumed to be nonexistent (determinism) and this conceit is never thought through properly, in its full implications, never followed to its source. And so there arise clever notions within a limited area, that eventually undermine the whole of human life. When their harmfulness is finally discovered, they generally cannot be reversed.

With the theme of the truly collective subconscious we return to the question from the first chapter. The individual and putatively collective Jungian subconscious can be *noticed* by normal consciousness just because it is not collective and because most people are not afflicted by it in the same or in a similar manner ("noticing" here is still a long way from understanding or being able to treat). It emerges into clear consciousness in one way or another–pathologically, in dreams, in fantasies–and is noticed because it differs from what today is considered as normal. But if something works its way into normal consciousness as a truly collective inspiration, then this consciousness, conditioned by centuries of such inspirations, cannot recognize it, and it appears as a self-evident, obvious idea, as philosophy, as scientific theory. Such an "idea" is recognized as a subconscious inspiration only by a consciousness that providentially has not been infected by it or has at least partially conquered its pathology through a schooling of consciousness.

Every psychological illness, especially the deepest, collective illness, is self-sealing, i.e., it is itself the greatest obstacle to its own healing. The realization that the idea of matter is an anti-idea, an unconcept, is prevented above all by the idea itself, by its subconscious power. Once an unthinkable but psychologically powerful "thought" is accepted into thinking consciousness, it has a paralyzing effect on the other areas of thought. Thus the resistance of the autonomous consciousness vis-à-vis the individual subconscious is weakened as well. Probably many psychical illnesses only become possible on the basis of the collective illness.

Investigating the state of affairs of mental illness does not leave one with a very comforting picture. Individual psychical disease may be noticed, and the sufferer may turn to a doctor, and with luck the doctor may even help him. But how and where and to whom should a collectively diseased mankind turn for its cosmic doctor, since the disease itself goes unnoticed? And yet it lies within each person's freedom to identify the disease, and to discover that the healing principle is present within himself: his Logos-essence. Until now the soul was passive; it suffered what happened to it at the hands of humanity's pedagogy or counter-forces. Its healing starts with the insight that it can be active and that it is capable of building an active psyche in the place of its passively imagined non-cognizing forms, its subconscious inspirations. This more active soul will not be turned back at the boundary of the supra-conscious, but will penetrate and enrich the spiritual world with human creation.

CHAPTER FOUR

Remembering and Forgetting

In the course of the individual life-span, as in the evolutionary history of mankind, formative and sensitive forces are released from the subtler parts of the human organism. Before becoming free, they form the body, they effect its growth, and they work particularly on the formation of the corporeal organs of cognitive life. To the extent that they complete their bodily task, their liberation is brought about by the gradual incarnation of the individuality, of the thinker and speaker in man, as the latter unites with the organism. Birth, learning to speak and think, the second teeth, sexual maturity–these are stages in the incarnation of the higher man. This incarnation proceeds continually up to the midpoint of life, when excarnation begins. The self-incarnating Logos-being takes–or should take–responsibility for both the organism and the forces that are freed. The latter *could* become cognitive forces; that would be their legitimate role. And they did so in earlier times under the guidance of the "gods." Called perceptual- and thinking-forces in the preceding chapters, they appear as limit-experiences and, if not taken up appropriately by man, become the substance of the subconscious. In the universal realm where these processes reign, the distinction between inner and outer has no meaning, and so it is possible (and appropriate) to portray these same forces from two standpoints on the level of mirrored consciousness.

Also to be counted among those formative forces that spoil if they do not become conscious for the individual are the forces of destiny, tied to both the bodily and the subtler organism. The growth of "the Logos that belongs to the soul" sets in motion the life- and sensitive-forces of man; as universal forces, they can at all times mediate the limit-experiences that are beginning to be conscious and also the universal knowledge beyond these limits.

What is noticeable during life in a general way—the liberation of growth- and sensitive-forces, their transformation into cognitive forces—occurs on a small scale in every cognitive act. In every cognition in which the nervous system plays a part, a little death occurs in the latter which is then partially reversed in the course of the next sleep. But the subtler parts of the rhythmic and metabolic systems are also affected in every cognitive act. This is why both systems also play a part in remembering.

The incarnation of the true I, of the speaker and thinker in us, consists in this subject building itself an *I-organism* out of the forces that are beginning to be free. This organism does not separate it from the universal processes, which continue within the liberated forces, thus making cognition possible. The liberation of forces takes place in a different way and to a different degree in the three systems of the body: the forces are most free in the head-system, less so in the rhythmic, and least of all in the metabolic- and limb-system. But all forces cooperate in the processes of cognition and memory.

The participation of the entire body in pro-cesses of memory can be seen in the fact that our capa-city for memory is strongly influenced, whether helped or hindered, by the condition of the body (e.g. tiredness), by one's life-situation (e.g. dis-ease), by mood, and by the person's will. These cir-cumstances can be correctly observed only if the var-ious forms of "memory" are sharply distinguished and separately considered. They can then also be brought into relation with one another.

The fundamental phenomenon of specifically human memory consists in this: something that we have thought or perceived or mentally pictured is lifted, repeatedly and at will, into consciousness again. This process is performed many times in a day by humans, mostly without being noticed or regis-tered as memory. It becomes noticeable and con-scious when impeded, e.g. when something "slips our mind"–a word, a name, etc.

At the other end of the hierarchy of memory-processes there lies the phenomenon of obsessional thoughts or images that occupy consciousness with-out the will, or even against the will, of the subject. Between these two extremes we can observe other kinds of remembering: the recognition of something previously encountered; unwilled associative re-membering, remembering something that has been "memorized," etc.

Willed, active remembering is a specifically human capacity for two reasons. On earth, only man has the use of a will directed by an I; we could even say, this capacity for willing *is* the I. This capacity is also the capacity for thinking, since only what is specified in thought can be willed by the I. But what has been specified in thought and remembered is a *that*–and a *that* means something wordlike, or a word. The capacity for speaking–in words–is closely bound to the capacity for remembering: the one cannot be imagined without the other.

According to the scientific view most often presented, even though consciousness may be directed to various other contents, every experience becomes *stored* somehow, e.g. in the mind or in the brain. When remembered, the stored elements are elevated into consciousness once again. Now let us review more closely this notion of a storage (perhaps encoded) of experience, be it of perceptual images, thoughts, or dreams. Let us assume there were a flawless and complete storage of "memories." Would this answer the question of the essence of memory, or even contribute to the answer? We now would face another, at least equally difficult question: How does the rememberer know *what* to choose, in any given case, from the multiplicity of what has been stored? Asking the question this way already suggests that the essential thing in remembering is precisely the ability to choose. But if one knows *what* to choose, one has already remembered it. Even in the case of an obstructed memory, there is certainty in this choosing capacity: the person who cannot think of a name or a thing still confidently rejects all incorrect attempts to reconstruct what has been forgotten–whether suggested by himself or others–and recognizes it with certainty once it is found.

The idea of stored experiences does not solve the problem of memory. And it leaves another question unanswered. Humans do not experience "data"–one unit of information after the other –rather, they experience in a continuum, polyphonically. For example, along with a given event, we also experience parallel thoughts, and those in the back of our mind, as well as feelings, memories, etc. "Storage" would have to occur accordingly, with no gradation, for example, according to importance or significance. In recollecting, a person would then have to choose from out of a multilayered series of data.

Active memory is not only linked, but *related* to the phenomenon of thinking in adults. One can distinguish between intuitive and consequential thinking. Through the former, new concepts are formed, or rather "beheld." Through the latter, relationships are presented among already-formed concepts. No sharp line can be drawn between these two kinds of thinking. Memory seems to be close to intuitive thinking. The latter can "find" *new* ideas that it has never thought before; the former can "find" thoughts and representational images that were in consciousness once before. If a person knows *what* is to be remembered then the memory has already occurred. The analogy in thinking is: if a person knows what he wants to think, then he has already thought it. In both cases, the willing and doing are identical, in contrast to other will-processes, in which a thought and its realization are separate. Choice is certain even in the case of blocked memory: the difficulty does not lie in the rememberer's not knowing what he wants; it is only that he cannot for the moment realize this *what*. But if he really didn't know what he were looking for at all, then no one could help him. An analogy in thinking: One is often incapable of solving a riddle, but one recognizes the correct solution with certainty.

Only what has been thought can be remembered actively, i.e. at will. To what extent feeling elements accompany this process depends only slightly, if at all, on the conscious will. This kind of remembering is equivalent to our capacity for the word. Only a *that*, a something, can be remembered in this way, and *that* is word, is wordlike. *To have thought* also implies the capacity for the word. Only a *speaking* being can actively remember. The more intensively something was thought, the more easily it can be remembered at will. This is also the reason memorized texts are harder to remember than, for example, trains of thought that one makes up oneself. Unfamiliar trains of thought would have to be thought through with the same absorption as one's own in order for them to be remembered in the same way. For texts, the memory of specific words is also necessary. Today, we experience words and think them in a very different way than thoughts; the consciousness for the word is much more dreamlike, much less sharply delineated, and for us the thought and the word almost never coincide completely.

Today, consciousness in Western man is always movement; moving or being moved, it becomes consciousness—in becoming a given content or un-becoming on the way to a different content. If consciousness does not live in this conscious becoming and un-becoming, then it is not self-consciousness, but dream-consciousness or archaic consciousness or even associative consciousness, which is certainly in constant motion, but not according to the will. The content at any given moment, with which consciousness has identified, ceases to be *that*; it returns to the more fluid element from which it was born, out of which it became *that* particular content. It returns to the *process*, in which thinking still lives without words or signs, but in words of a higher order—a process the human being does not know of because his consciousness lights up with the *result* of the process, with its past. *That* returns to the *continuity* from which it was removed, and it is preserved by a concept, which is its potential, the grave of its living being, to await the act of remembering that resurrects it.

Concepts and concept-related forms—e.g. sense-qualities—cannot be repeated in consciousness mechanically. That would be neither memory nor a gesture of human consciousness at all. Conceptuality must be understood; it cannot be either imitated or reproduced without comprehension: we would not know *what* we are quoting. When recollecting a representational formation, the conceptuality is the guide that lifts it into consciousness: we have to conceive of *what* it is.

Active remembering is an intuitive act, except that the intuition is not happening for the first time, since consciousness has already practiced the gesture or form of movement in question. In other words, it is not that the content of the memory has been stored, but rather that the structure of the person's consciousness has been changed by the first thinking or perceiving. The *functional change* in the attention's capacity for movement makes the second, third, etc. discovery of the concept easier than it was at its first formation.

Obviously, only a someone, an I, can remember actively, intentionally. They are *my* memories; there can be no question of an impersonal storage, although that is precisely the implication of the models of memory as storage. *I* know *what* I want to remember. Associative, mechanical "remembering" has nothing to do with real human memory. Just as a thought is only a thought for an *I*, thus it is for memory. The associative area of psychological and mental life does not belong to the part of consciousness controlled by the I, and has a disturbing effect on its autonomy.

The thinking and speaking I–not the ego, which wakes to consciousness with the already-thought or the already-spoken–lives in presentness, or the sphere of life, of intuitions. In consciousness, the human being shifts back and forth between I and ego, between present and past. In the past-phase, attention becomes *form*, the thought or perceived or represented form. In presence, the attention, the I lives form-free, *in* thinking, *in* perceiving, *in* representing something. The I, the attention, can assume all forms. If I follow someone's speech or text, I *become* his words, word by word; I *become*, by dissolving (reading) these words, his sentences, sentence by sentence; and by dissolving the sentences in a higher reading I *become*, thought-form by thought-form, his ideas, which are the source of his sentences and words. I do not remain in a final form; I stay free of forms; I can go on and think something new. The capacity for remembering thus consists in a functional trace, otherwise the I would have to preserve memories as *formed* structures, and then it would face the problem of choosing among them, which would raise the question of a second memory, which would lead to a third, etc. Even the functional formative capacity must not be too pronounced, or the forms acquire a life of their own and become part of the associative realm.

In the human being of today, conscious thinking penetrates as far as the physical organism; it causes processes there as well, as does conscious perceiving. In order to make experience conscious, past-consciousness needs the physical processes. They make up the resistance or contrast to the "imitative," identifying movement of the I, of the sensitivity, of the free living organism. Experience

–conscious experience–can only be had by the I, which participates in the physical organism by being partly identified with it.

The physical human body cannot be imagined without the liveliness, the sensitivity, the I-quality that form, sustain and enliven it. Even the physical body is not entirely sealed off in its form, but is subject to a continual interchange with the surrounding air, water, and earth, even with heat. The life-*body* and the sensitivity-*body*, in a narrower sense, are the non-free regions of the organism; they are bound to the being and functioning of the physical body. Man's cognitive and creative functions are effected by the areas of life and sensitivity that are free, or become free, for the cognitive, speaking I-being. The "formed" part of the I is called the ego, and is its non-cognitive part, through which the I-being identifies itself with the bodily-living-psychical organism, putting down roots there. What is non-cognitive in the human organism is necessary in order to make conscious what is perceived by the free, cognitive part of the human being–i.e., the part that identifies itself with the *that*, with the cognitive "object." As it becomes *that*, the free I is transformed entirely, the sensitivity more restrainedly, and the life-sphere even less. The last two are closely tied to their pre-formed, biologically and reflexively active portions, into which they tend to merge. Of these, the biological is more definitely formed than the corresponding sensitivity, just as a plant is more strictly a living *form* than an animal, which is a sensitive or instinctual form: The animal adapts perfectly to its environment, within the limits of its range of sensitivity.

What goes on in the free part of the human being is a universal process. The paralysis of these processes results from the unfree, formed part of the human being. Thereby a part of the world process becomes conscious as it surges around us, a part of the interchange between the world of light and the human essence. Normally, we call "world" the part of this exchange that has become conscious, the "thought-world," the "perceptual world." What has remained unconscious has, in youth, a formative effect on the organism, on the organs of cognition, and later in life on one's fate and on the individual and collective subconscious–unless it be raised into consciousness to some extent by means of a schooling of consciousness.

An animal's sensitivity is the immediate "awareness" of its vital situation, which includes conditioning circumstances from far beyond its physical body. Such sensitivity is therefore incapable of memory. Animal "remembering," e.g. in the case of conditioned reflex, consists in the exercise of species-specific, biologically significant connections or, in young animals, connections that come about in play. Plants do not "learn," even in this sense. In man, the unfree sensitivity and aliveness do not play an immediate role in remembering. An effect is brought about in the life-body and the sensitive-body only because, in order to become conscious, thought or percept has to penetrate into the nervous system. Remembering is a capacity of the I, and it is based on a functional alteration extending to the body, through the agency of the free life-energies and free sensitivity.

The role of these free forces is differentiated according to their origin: whether they have been liberated in the head-system, the rhythmic system, or the metabolic-limb-system. In the process of remembering, it is the free energies from the lower two systems that play the major part. What has been liber-ated with regard to the head-system becomes active for thinking, in thought-intuition; and for perceiving, in perceptual intuition. We can look at perception as an intuition that the I receives, but that the I does not produce or cause. Something analogous can be said for thought-intuition, although here consciousness generally plays an incomparably more active role than in perceiving, where the sense organs are used.

In the case of active memory, the outer source of either a thought or a percept is lacking. An inner source is activated by the will of the I: this source is to be found in the free energies liberated from the two lower systems. They took part in thinking and in perceiving, and so exercised a certain gesture, by adapting themselves to their object. This gesture does not correspond to the content of perceiving and thinking become conscious, but to what remained supraconscious in the act of cognition. What became conscious was paralyzed, lost its liveliness. What does not become conscious retains its life and causes, or is, the functional change in the free energy -systems that originate in the rhythmic and metabolic systems.

Normally, this effect does not result from a lasting formation, but rather from the living possibility of grasping *at will* and more *easily* the same thoughts or percepts, as an intuition, for the second time–or repeatedly. In the intuition, the will stays free, it does not enter into the effect. In order to make memory conscious, the whole movement, which starts from the I and ensues through the I-like movement of free sensitivity- and life-energies, reaches right into the physical body. Difficulties in remembering generally arise at this point in the process: the physical body offers resistance. This is why a person can "know" whether or not a word is the "right one" or not, even though he cannot overcome the blockage in the nervous system.

The supraconscious interplay between the liberated energies of the human being and the part of the world that remains unconscious does not normally result in the formation of a lasting structure on the part of these energies–not, that is, to the extent that thinking or perceiving goes on in clear consciousness, modeled by the I. Should this not be the case, however, should not everything become conscious that could be consciously experienced–for emotional, egotistical, or intellectual reasons (the problem of limit experiences)–then once again forms are built up within the liberated forces that lead a separate life, removed from the I, beneath the level of consciousness. This subconscious region of the soul is distinguished from the supraconscious by its very formed-ness. In the normal process of memory, the formal energy must not remain undissolved: this is what makes up the free function of active remembering. When the memories stand still, as fixed forms, they become part of the associative sphere or, in the worst case, turn into obsessional representations. If an energy belonging to man is liberated and withdraws from the control of the I or the I's representative, it becomes form once more, but under the sign of egotism or of anti-human forces, hostile to the word, whose style in everyday life and human relationships is not to be overlooked. The established energy-forms distort memory, as they distort the objective course of thinking and perceiving.

The discussion of cognitive processes requires the formation of new concepts that are qualitatively different from the concepts of everyday consciousness: for example, the concepts "life," "I," "ego," "sensitivity." It is advisable to understand these concepts in a purely functional way, as processes, rather than tying them down substantively, which is often a mistake even at the level of everyday consciousness. It is also important to give the concept "form" qualitatively different meanings at its various levels, e.g. the living form and the form of sensitivity.

Human attention is autonomous; a person can even intentionally direct it away from present circumstances. This capacity implies at the same time

the capacity for active remembering, the intentional
liberation from the current inner and outer circumstances. Animals clearly lack this capacity: an animal constantly lives in the present moment, and its
world is limited by its sensitive form, which is the
animal itself. Current circumstances may awaken a
reflex-like "remembering" in the animal. The capacity for human, active memory is based on the
human being's past-consciousness, however. This
means not only that it begins with the already-
thought or the already-perceived, but also that the
human being experiences in clear consciousness
only what is already past, and experiences what is
present in a dull, dream-like way, apart from the rare
phenomenon of "presence of mind." When something new and unexpected happens to a person,
something he has not already experienced many
times–e.g. an accident nearby–then the experience
acquires sharp contours only *afterwards*, in remi-
niscing, and generally the memory differs considerably from the actual event. The memory of dreams
is similar. The animal is locked into the current
course of events by means of its "dream-consciousness." Through his past-consciousness, the human
being is in a position to distance himself from current events.

Temporal presence is a contradiction in terms.
In time only past and future exist, the latter as an
extrapolation, onto what has not yet happened, of
the flow of time that man experiences only in its
past form. Essential presence intersects with the

world of time in the single point of so-called temporal presence. Whoever experiences this point knows
that it is merely the point of contact between
eternal presence and time.

Eternal, lasting presence is the sphere of life experienced in its sensitivity-light; it is the site, the
world, where living thinking and feeling, as well as
everything "past," are present in their figurative
image. This means that we have to reconsider our
"standpoint": it is not that the "past," the "dead"
for example, "go away" or are not *there*; rather, it is
we who–because of our past-consciousness–are not
there where they are, in eternal presence. Through
thought-intuition, through memory, we take part in
this world. For contemporary man, it is both
individual and cosmic. He experiences his individual
world of presence as a tableau when in mortal danger or at other moments when the connection of his
"life" with his physical body becomes loosened. The
schooling of consciousness brings the possibility of
experiencing both the individual, lasting presence,
that we normally call "past," and also the cosmic
presentness in various degrees. For the latter experience, it is necessary to let the I-quality, which normally leans on the physical body, become so strong
within itself that it can dispense with both the physical body and the individually experienced life, and
go on to experience itself in the free part of its sensitivity. Individual and cosmic "history" blend into
one another; they are only distinct during earthly
life.

It must be emphasized that the latter portrayal of memory is not different from what preceded it. What was described as the "functional capacity" for repetition of an intuition or representation *is* at the same time the reality of presentness: there are no "things," no "facts" there; but rather life, living thoughts, images, events. The portrayal of the soul's realities will necessarily sound paradoxical to the onesided past-consciousness.

Active remembering is, understandably, not a very ancient achievement of the human being. Earlier, "remembering" was much more a re-presentation in the true sense, a re-experiencing of events, an ability to enter into eternal presence, into lived situations. There was no great difference between the first experience and the "memory." Past-consciousness was developed only in the elect, and in them often merely in preparatory form. As late as the time of Christ, bearing "witness" was not simply utterance, but a re-enlivening and a making-experienceable of the witnessed contents, which *convinced* –otherwise they were not valid. This is shown in the difficulty of finding "correct" false witnesses against Jesus. Hand in hand with the fading of the capacity for re-experience in presence–as the individual formative life-energies became more independent–there appeared a dampening in perception that has continued into our own time. Earlier, remembrance could be a re-enlivening of perception, because perception was itself alive. Today, memory is more a reproduction *in thought* of experienced or thought contents; in any case, it begins with thought. Even when mental images are remembered, this does not take place immediately, but is introduced through conceptu-ality. Since in earlier times the latter arose in man through a perception that was not yet completely separated from thinking (from what we *now* call thinking), an immediate *image-memory* was still possible. It could be called imaginative memory. The shift in the character of memory toward a thinking wordlike direction corresponds to the transformation from an earlier Light-experience toward Logos-experience: a transformation in keeping with the Judaeo-Christian spiritual evolution. To the extent that a person does not speak out of present intuition, out of meditation, he always expresses past-contents. For this, memory and word-language are necessary–not a language with improvised elements and rules, as was the primal language (a language of vowels). For active memory, words have to be there with approximately fixed, approximately constant meanings. This is why active memory has been possible ever since man has begun to speak in word-languages–even though there are not words for everything that is remembered, and even though new thoughts are born wordlessly, in accordance with the higher word.

If modern man wants to remember higher cognitions, he cannot rely on normal memory, since higher cognition unfolds in the context of a renunciation of the physical nervous system. Memory has to become largely similar to ancient memory: the "representing" of what has been experienced, which is "sought out" for a second time. It is always problematic to bridge the gulf between the consciousness of a word-language, in which the experience has to be expressed, and the consciousness of higher experience. The utterance is never unambiguous, and has to be received very actively, through thought-intuition; otherwise it will inevitably lead to misunderstanding.

If the way of active memory has been understood to some extent, then the functioning of the more passive kinds of memory becomes easier to understand. The re-cognition of what has already once been thought or perceived, when it is encountered again, is analogous to active memory; only the process is not instigated directly by the will–rather, the will is itself activated by the new percept. In perception, the I and the free part of the sensitivity go along with the process to a large extent. The life-form becomes slightly loosened thereby, and is given the possibility of intuitively finding the corresponding concept.

Purely associative "memory" is actually a wide-spread symptom of diseased consciousness: it is the very image of biological reflexes in animals or humans, though clothed as thought. It belongs to the realm of ready-made, already-thought thoughts that can be copied, and which a person does not think anew but uses as *stored, encoded signs*. The idea of stored memories is based on this type of memory: precisely on the non-human in man. It should be emphasized again that in cases of storage, the memories themselves (what has been experienced) cannot be sought directly, but rather their signs, the encoded signs. As we have seen, in active memory it is the content itself that is consciously and directly chosen; there is no trace of representative signs in consciousness: it proceeds in an exactly opposite way to the computer.

Unintentional, associative "memories" are always very emotionally laden; in extreme cases, there is barely any thought content, but rather overall feelings of discomfort, disgust, or pleasant sensations, that crops up in a particular place or situation. In memory-tests, it is almost exclusively associative memory–only rarely used in normal life–that is being investigated. Even when it *is* used, what is remembered has a thought-significance, in contrast to remembering completely meaningless syllables, as required in the relevant research.

In our time, man tends toward very incomplete perception and even such perception is sought by him in excess, relative to what he is able to think through. Passive abandonment mainly to emotionally charged visual images or sound-images of mainly emotional appeal is not "union" of the I with what has been experienced. It is not the I, but the sensitive-body that "perceives" and "remembers" accordingly. Instead of union through the I there arises a psychological adhering to the incompletely received percept. This phenomenon signals a regression to the anachronistic psychological gesture of the sensitive soul, and like every regression it is accompanied by a sense of mental and psychological pleasure: hence the attraction of this attitude.

The phenomenon of "déjà vu"–recognition of a situation in feeling, but without conceptual ripeness–suggests important conclusions as to the deeper processes of remembering and forgetting. The feeling, "that's familiar," arises through a functional formation of the sensitivity, supraconsciously stamped into it by the I. This stamping does not penetrate to the "life" and therefore not to the physical level either–otherwise we would remember "concretely," i.e. as formulated in *thoughts*. It is characteristic that this experience often occurs in dreams, during which the connection between the I and the sensitivity on the one hand, and between the physical organism and the life-body on the other, is considerably loosened.

Every memory is a local, transitory loosening of the life from the physical organism, and so there is a parallel transitory destruction of physical life for the sake of spiritual life. If the life in the human being is loosened more intensively than during memory, whether through sickness, tribulation, fear, sense of danger, or fasting, etc., then the "visions" and "voices" may arise that have been described in monastic literature for centuries. These psychologically and mentally very real experiences stem from an unusual enlivening of memory-images, of representations. Typically, they do not portray any new intuitions or cognitions; their content could be reproduced as representation, save that in this case the representations are *alive* and have the stamp of reality. If the life body is loosened to an extreme, as in immediate mortal danger, then the person often sees his whole life spread before him in a single continuous image: experientially, we could say that it is spread out before him in space. It is not a question of static representational images, nor even of "individual" images at all, but of a total view, a simultaneous grasp of the whole life, a kind of tableau-experience.

Active memory can be comprehended as a pinpoint tableau-experience. It is an activity that proceeds in polar opposition to the life of the senses. If something is to become an experience for us, it has to touch on the physical body, and a functional change has to occur in all essential articulations of the human being, so that memory becomes possible as a second or repeated intuition. The intuition, as well as its memory, is body-free–whether it be an intellectual or a perceptual intuition. Still, in memory, the point of orientation for the will that seeks to remember is a *functional trace* in the whole organism, even in its bodily aspect. This trace is caused by the part of the experience that does not become conscious–by the other side of the world of thoughts and percepts, the side which we normally never see.

Just as normal thinking is a pinpoint realization of living, imaginative thinking, a lightening flash from that realm, and just as normal perception is a flash of living, imaginative perception, so too the activity of fantasy vision is immediate "image-form-ing," i.e. immediate image-making activity, a flash of the original live representing. Normal representation arises with the help of a thought, a concept; in the vision, image (including sound-image) is not separated from conceptuality–all three activities of consciousness have their imaginative levels.

Healthy memory is tied to healthy *forgetting*. If thoughts or images are too rigidly formed they cannot be forgotten and therefore can also not be actively remembered; they acquire independence, and in extreme cases, become obsessive representations. If the formation is too feeble, we have pathological forgetfulness. In the independent zone of the soul, in the domain of association, we are dealing with a past that influences, through its undissolved persistence, both the present and the future. It is clear that experiences should not pass over us without a trace; as *capacities*, they should enrich our lives, our potentials. If they remain as independent inclusions within us, as fixed forms of psychological life, then they compromise our new, present potential for experience. Hence, the exercises for the dissolution of "habits" are important also on grounds of mental and psychological hygiene.

Man is dualistically inclined: the earthly man is linked with the heavenly man, with the one "from above"–the lower trinity with the higher trinity. Where they overlap there arises the formation of the "I." Dualism–apparent in all human activities, capacities, achievements–is present only to be overcome. Overcoming it does not mean denying or dismissing one pole. Man breathes more or less rhythmically, always between two poles: in memory and forgetting between formation and dissolution; between past consciousness and present consciousness; between waking and sleeping; between being-in-oneself and being surrendered to another; between intuition and becoming conscious of intuition. This rhythmic nature gives him the possibility of *noticing* both poles and *knowing* them, becoming conscious of both of them. This is why he can conceive of past *and* present, determinism *and* freedom: because he belongs neither wholly to one nor wholly to the other pole; he takes part in both. The Manvantaras and Pralayas of his remembering and forgetting gradually educate him into a true I-being, in whose contemplation duality is not experienced as eliminated but rather surpassed, transcended; identity and at the same time experience of identity.

CHAPTER FIVE

The Image of the Soul

A Summary

Two kinds of activity are possible for thinking consciousness: thinking can be used in order to understand something–something perceived or thought–or else thinking can turn toward itself. The latter possibility is at once the beginning of, and the capacity for, psychology. Introspection begins with what is now the most illumined psychological faculty, deepens itself there, and spreads out ever further over the neighboring areas, illuminating them in turn.

By observing itself, thinking achieves two insights: first of all, it learns that what is observed is the past, one's own past, the result of prior, unnoticed processes of thinking or perceiving; second, it learns that this observation is only possible if the observing agency does not itself belong to the past: there is a past only for someone present. This present consciousness, which does not initially experience itself, becomes more and more tangible through the initial act of introspection, and the question arises in consciousness of how to make presence a more direct experience. Here lies the beginning of the path of consciousness-exercises. Observation of the most illumined soul-activity at the time is the preface, the introduction, to raising the observing capacity of consciousness to a higher level.

The secret of self-experience is the secret of the I. The I *is* the self-experience, which can be realized at various levels of consciousness: the primary step necessary for the foundation of a psychology was described in the first chapter. In the age of the consciousness soul, self-experience (not self-feeling) comes about, in its lowest form, as observation of the already-thought. Therefore it is important that introspection consists initially in looking at the cognitive gestures of consciousness, at its own past, since normally consciousness is incapable of observing non-cognitive elements of the soul, lacking sufficient objectivity for that purpose. Initially, it has autonomy with regard to its own past. What disturbs concentrated thinking, the associations that distract it, the feelings and passions, indicate the lower limits of this autonomy.

If we picture the realm of the already-thought as a specific zone in the soul, then we can characterize the next higher zone as the one from which the past is observed–initially without the observing center experiencing itself consciously. From this region there stem all new ideas and every new understanding. This presence is a living region, a continuity like that of non-enumerable understanding itself. This continuum breaks up into words and concepts. Vestigial traces of this life are revealed in the "meaning" of words, in the ability of concepts to be transformed and combined. Speaking (in the full sense of the term, "having something to say") as well as the speaker, are the source of the presentness, through which the world of the past is nourished and amplified as out of a living point-source. Speaking is itself nourished out of the sphere of life.

Above the sphere of life, with no demarcation between them, we find the zone of cognitive feeling, of original feeling. Its effects are felt in everyday consciousness as the feeling of evidence, of logicality, as aesthetic feeling, as the feeling of truth, as a feeling of the perceptual image. From this sphere originate inspirations of the good and the beautiful. It is especially the hearable (temporal) arts that come from this sphere; they reach the perceptual world without going through the imaginative world.

The world of cognitive willing reveals itself in everyday consciousness in a manner that clearly shows how, in the region of the soul above that of everyday consciousness, world-processes and soul-spiritual inner processes are neither different nor separate. For cognitive will appears above all in the existence or the givenness of the perceptual world–not in its being-thus, which depends on man–and in the givenness of the thinking process: *that* it happens. This will contains feeling and thinking; during their descent from the universal will into the human soul, they become separately experienced qualities.

The three higher spheres of the human soul–its life source–are supraconscious for everyday consciousness. They are normally accessible for the adult only rarely, momentarily, in a flash; generally, this access does not lie within human control. The human being is separated from the upper portion of the soul in part by the zone of the subconscious, which is formed in the course of life; and in part his consciousness is effaced through the weakness of the I-experience when he approaches the supraconscious individual. Children, on the other hand, are largely open to this world of the soul, in part because the subconscious is not yet formed and in part because consciousness still functions with no I-experi-ence–which only appears after acquisition of the essential elements for the capacity to speak and to think. Hence, the most important human capacities arise in the child supraconsciously: standing upright, speaking and thinking. Throughout life, these latter remain supraconscious capacities, to the extent that speaking and thinking are taken in the essential sense–to think something new, to say something new, or to do both with such concentration that they become improvised activities, independent of their content. The child knows nothing of the rules of his mother tongue–nor does the adult need to know them–and still less of the "rules" of thinking, whose essence remains generally hidden to the adult as well.

Supraconscious capacities are also acquired later on. Everything later becomes a supraconscious capacity that has first been very consciously learned and practiced: for example, writing and reading, abil-ities in the crafts or arts, all activities that have cog-nitive character or a wordlike, speaking nature.

Many sports abilities can be included here, to the extent that they do not rely on trained reflexes; the distinguishing characteristic is revealed in how they function in new situations. We can speak of habits of a higher kind, but these habits are always changeable. They actively adapt to the new; they correspond to cognition differently from normal habits, and they are always penetrable to consciousness; they remain capacities.

The formation of the various senses is an example of such habits. For instance, the sense of vocal sound or the sense of concept is initially only a sense organ for the quality of sound or of concept. Later, the sound-organism is built up out of the sounds that have been heard, the concept-organism is built out of the conceptualities that have been received, and the organisms thus formed become in turn sense organs themselves: the sounds or concepts that have already been built in can be understood with no need for mentation. These organisms, like any and all understanding, are formed in the supraconscious. These are capacities of the I.

The soul's supraconscious region can be described as that of the specifically human capacities. Because they are I-capacities, the corresponding kinds of activity are without form. For the same reason, the subconscious is also specifically human: because its forms are made up from the supraconscious, drawn from the I.

The supraconscious is lightlike and wordlike: every understanding and every possibility of utterance (originally one and the same essence) originate there. All too lucid for everyday consciousness, it was even called the "upper darkness," in contrast to the lower obscurity that separates man from the light. This region of light stands in readiness for the contemporary human being: by understanding higher "wordlikenesses," by the formation of ideas, he can know its existence and its character and can learn, through the appropriate exercises in consciousness, to live with a heightened consciousness in the otherwise supraconscious spheres. The ideas of the living, of the feeling, of the willing Word, or of the living, the feeling, the willing idea-world, have to be formed in study and so precede their direct experience.

Word, language, cognition, can only come from above, from a source that lies higher than their own level. The higher aspects of the human being, as realities existing from the beginning, but still largely entrusted to creative entities and not yet taken over by mankind, are the corresponding sources of wordlike abilities and activities. All of these are of a nonprivate nature, just as ordinary thinking, perceiving, knowing and speaking have to do with the world and are therefore not subjective phenomena. The higher human capacities are intersubjective and relate in each case to realities that are also intersubjective. But intersubjective reality forms a *world*. And so living thinking, cognitive feeling, and cognitive willing lead into worlds that are not directly perceptible through the sense-organs, but whose effects are to be found within the perceptual world. We can call these worlds, collectively, the spiritual world, and we can call spiritual capacities those that belong to our being's more elevated components. If the soul becomes conscious in the latter, the human evolves from a soul-being to a spiritual being. The transition occurs between consciousness-soul and spirit-self. "The path that otherwise only leads to the soul, with the soul showing its outer surface, drives, and desires, leads us into the eternal soul, which is in us and penetrated with spirit, as spiritual as the spiritual environment. Now we can enter the region where the soul is one with the spirit." (Lecture of 6.5.22).

In its higher articulations and capacities, the human essence flows into a spiritual world common to all mankind. The higher components *are* in this world; they are not sharply separated from their "spiritual environment" as the bodily being is separated from the physical world by the mineral body; without the support of creative entities they would merge into this environment. The path of exercise for man has the goal of giving these higher articulations of being ever more wordlike borders, i.e., permeable, transphonic borders, such as words have: by itself, one word or one concept is not a reality, but only in a language or in a net of concepts, in living connection with other words and concepts, without relinquishing their singularity. Therefore man operates in meditation or in higher thought-intuition within a common sphere by which all men live and breathe. This gives meditation its special importance.

Since the supraconscious sphere is cognitive, a continuum of graduated possibilities of understanding, it is form-free, a flowing transparency. The capacity to remember something consciously understood is written into this element. As portrayed in the preceding chapter, it is no fixed form; rather, it makes functionally easier the repeated grasp of something whose non-conscious energetic form–its negative, we could say–was inscribed into the corresponding world of eternal presence. A similar situation exists in the case of the previously mentioned supraconscious capacities (speaking, thinking, acting, etc.) that are included in the supraconscious, as long as they are *capacities* and not fixed habits.

Below the layer of past thinking begins the region of the subconscious. The terms "sub" and "supra" have metaphorical meaning at most, and characterize the opposite "directions" of the two regions from the standpoint of everyday consciousness.

The associative, the uppermost layer of the subconscious, is distinguished from thinking and from the conceptual organism by the fact that in association the connection of concepts, representations, words and feeling-forms is not cognitive, but proceeds according to subjective experience. This is always directed toward what is "good for me." Thoughts, feelings, will-impulses, representations, form a conglomerate consisting of the formations that have become independent. Everything that has separated from the I-being, everything not consciously grasped by this being, falls into a self-contained, separate form that generally does not correspond to reality, since it does not correspond to cognition either. Since the corresponding contents have not been experienced consciously, or not completely so, they retain more "life" and "energy" than what has become conscious. Hence their power and effect over conscious mental life. Whatever does not remain as capacity, nor is grasped consciously by the I as a content, forms itself into the subconscious.

Subconscious formations arose from energies and capacities that originally belonged to the supraconscious region. They are formed for two reasons: because man encounters a great deal, of which only a fragment is perceived consciously; and because what has not been consciously perceived is managed or taken care of less and less by the creative powers that are entrusted with the higher components of the human being. The latter development was occasioned by the "withdrawal of the gods" from man. Human effort and devotion could have compensated for this loss by placing the energies released by the gods under their protection through cult and ritual; or else through conscious and willed further development of one's own consciousness, which the liberated energies also make possible. Both possibilities were disdained by the majority of mankind when they gave up the idea of the Logos or the Son, which is the essence of Christianity. We have good reason to assume that the subconscious began to be a

common formation during the Romantic period
–though certain individuals were always ahead of
their time.

Everything to be found in this region of the
soul is pre-formed and non-cognitive. We could put
it this way: Just as the physical body has form and is
non-cognitive but for this very reason provides the
necessary background for human cognition and action, so too the formed soul-quality is the body of
the soul. The expressions "etheric body," and "astral
body" point to this state of affairs, along with which
there also exist free life-energies and free sensitive-
energies that open the way for human cognition, and
by their wordlike nature make freedom possible.

Human advancement is possible just because of
the ongoing liberation of these energies, which are
entirely bound to the body in both the newborn baby
and in early man. And to the extent that the liberated energies are taken up neither by religious nor by
cognitive life, the formation of the subconscious
becomes possible.

What composes the subconscious could be
called "habit" in the broadest sense. The distinction
between capacities and habits becomes topical with
regard to supraconscious and subconscious. The habits of the subconscious extend from association to
those ways of behaving that are, within limits,
adaptable and changeable, those patterns of reaction
that possess a particular shape, a specific character,
even before they acquire their familiar form, e.g., before being formulated–on occasion through contact

with psychology–into words and concepts. Freud was entirely correct to this extent, that these formations always come about under the sign of egotism.

Although the formation of half-conscious and subconscious psychological forms takes place in the individual's soul life, and even as a result of predispositions linked to one's individual destiny, the forms bear many collective traits. This evokes the thought that the tendency for form has a *style* and therefore a power or energy determining a style. What we know of the emergence of egotism points in this direction. This does not mean that the subconscious leads to a common human sphere after the manner of the supraconscious. Rather, its commonality is effected instead by its extreme contagiousness, particularly by representations that put their stamp and form on the liberated energies of life and sensitivity. These forms are infectious, and are effortlessly accepted by their victim–while the ideas and impulses stemming from the supraconscious cannot be received without effort.

In early times, human pedagogy consisted largely in dealing with the liberated energies in a religious way. In part, rites and customs accompanied individual life; in part, the entire religious life (the experienceable and experienced reality for man of those times) underwent alteration epoch by epoch –in close accordance with the change in the particular constellations that were a valid sign of humanity's direction for that given period of time: from Gemini to Taurus, from Taurus to Aries. The liberated energies bore the stamp of divine powers, be they friendly, or–as always during the transition from one constellation to the next–hostile to humanity. Their supersensible reality determined earthly sensual life, or it was at least one reality together with the earthly–precisely the reality of the divine figures, their garment. These figures developed capacities in people by the force of their example, or they were the mirror for the dangers they faced: As an initiate, the human being could imagine them, could imaginatively give form to them, to the aspect of the world or of cognition that they represented as *capacities*. Non-initiates could gradually translate the received mythological image into individual capacities, and above all experience individuality itself, since the divine figures were individuals. Once a people or a part of humanity is sufficiently individualized, then polytheism is exchanged for monotheism. The Christian trinity as well is the threefold form of appearance–important for further self-knowledge–of a single godhead. And so soul experiences of divine figures or symbolic images surfacing today have altogether different meaning for the long-since individualized human being of our time than they did for earlier humanity. For us, they are not *spiritual* experiences; neither the experiencing subject nor the psychologist can regard them as spiritual capacities, and they lack the relationship to the wordlike that was the essence of the ancient divine figures. For the new energies that are being liberated today they have no significance, or no

positive significance. Nor are they any more collective than envy, ambition, or jealousy.

What was originally called the subconscious–by analytic psychology appropriate to that
time–today has become a largely conscious form of
life, justified and recommended by medicine and science. The subhuman posture of the soul, spreading
further by contagion, asserts itself more and more
strongly against traditionally received human val-
ues, which are now in retreat. The soul's tendency
toward these formerly subconscious forms is itself
an "inspiration" from this region. Like almost every
modern scientific achievement, analytic psychology
was a double-edged sword: depending on how it is
used, it can show man what he is not, or it can con-
vince him that he is what it shows–and he then becomes accordingly. Only a new insight into one's
own nature and potential, based not on tradition but
on current knowledge of a higher kind, could prevent the subconscious sphere from determining life
more and more completely.

Gradually, a "world" is described by the out-
wardly induced, infectious collective construction of
forms (a "world" because it is intersubjective).
Added to this there is the truly collective unconscious, which stems from limit-experiences appropriate to, but dismissed by contemporary humanity:
subconscious "inspirations" arise that could be
called collective. As an example, in addition to what
has already been mentioned, we could take the loss
of the idea of the Logos, which was a common limit-

experience at the time of Christ and in the following few centuries. It was lost early on in the Church, approximately in the 4th Century. Then came the Mohammedan-Arabic counterstrike, with the central theme: Allah has no son–the denial of the idea of the Son or Logos. From this source there stems today's most wide-spread disease of consciousness: the ongoing "forgetting" of current, present thinking or utterance, behind the thought or spoken content. This makes possible the attitude of self-repudiation in which the human being, thinking, and spirit alike deny themselves by deriving themselves from something that is non-conscious. This reductionism is an inspiration with roots in sensitivity: the "inspiration" to deny the Word proceeds from not having grasped the idea of the Logos.

Inspirations of this kind, to the extent they are collective, are recognized as such by very few people; it becomes more and more difficult to tell them apart from inspirations coming from above. We see this in art as well. Even the distinction of the associative from the intuitive is, at least theoretically, difficult–perhaps not for mathematics, but particularly in art. What has been subconsciously inspired is always effective, infectious, through its content of sensitivity. It is well known that only the cognitive feeling of evidence is decisive in questions of truth, and precisely this feeling is diseased by subconscious inspirations: this is the disease, and constitutes its self-sealing character. Naturally, pure thinking can always distinguish association from intuition, but through the disease of consciousness, such thinking itself becomes ever more rare. Subconscious "sensitivity," which remains from those contents not grasped by consciousness in thought, and which becomes attached to induced representations, is just as effective as cognitive feeling would be; they are hardly to be differentiated theoretically. Nor is realizability a distinguishing characteristic, since the "subconscious" realizes itself to a very high degree, even becoming a justified form of life, with its own style, claims and satisfactions. The picture seems to be hopeless, if we disregard one important characteristic of the soul.

Up to now, we have found six functions: thinking, feeling and willing, each either in its free, cognitive, or pre-formed, non-cognitive aspects. The latter make up a conglomerate that consists of swirling movement; the former interpenetrate in such a way that the higher element sends impulses into the lower element. The *I-experience* of man is to be regarded today as a continual *movement* of the attention, which dwells most noticeably in the already-thought but also moves up into the living, to see the past from out of presentness. Because the Iexperience, like consciousness, ignites on contact with the past, which it must "experience" from out of the present, however, it can be represented as a contin-ual alternation between the cognizing and the non-cognizing. It can come about as I-experience neither by remaining in cognizing nor in noncognizing.

Every understanding, every formation of a concept, every intuition, comes from the higher, cognitive part, from the supraconscious. From the lower part come associations, emotions, sympathies, antipathies, and will-impulses of an unfree nature. Through a schooling of cognitive faculties, man learns to be gradually more *contemplative*, becoming conscious and self-conscious while dwelling in the supraconscious.

The I-experience in its egoic form is the human being's strongest drive. But this means that his attention must initially be in motion between the various layers of the soul. To even feel himself as an I, the human must have contact with presence, with the sphere of life. And that gives him the possibility of one day awakening in regard to his awareness, i.e., he can achieve intuitions with regard to his situation, his subjection to the lower element. As long as the need for I-experience is there, man has hope. He can take his fate into his own hands.

The rhythm of I-experience remains predominantly in the region of everyday consciousness. But this excludes neither inspirations and intuitions of the very highest, nor impulses of the very lowest. Though they may seem to swamp the I completely, it is part of the nature of *human* instincts and passions that they still require an experiencing or sensitive subject. As long as the I-experience is not "given up" through excessive misuse of the organism, it will always re-emerge, in its painfulness, from out of the sensitive "experience" in the lower zone. It can even happen that a being learns from this to seek out the path towards the real human. Much depends on what other people bring to the sphere of universal life through their meditation.

The psychologist, his scientific consciousness generally trained and exercised in grasping things on the level of the past, must learn to see the phenomenal form and the essence of the I in the "how" of attention's movements. Desiring to understand the supraconscious, he is confronted with the necessity of forming further ideas of a higher quality. To accomplish this task, he can begin by trying to see, in the how of a phenomenon, a more powerful and higher reality than in its content. Thus he will gradually be able to draw on the supraconscious to heal the subconscious. For this is what healing the soul really means.

CHAPTER SIX

Afterword

"There is no true psychology that does not begin with imaginative contemplation." This sentence is a special expression of a general epistemological law that, to be sure, is seldom followed in the sciences: a problem can be neither understood nor solved from the same level of consciousness on which it lies, but only from the standpoint of a higher level. The fulfillment of this law was the key that opened the way for these researches. Their themes resulted from personal affinity and general relevance: the method of procedure was always observation. The latter may begin in the direction taken by Rudolf Steiner's *Philosophy of Freedom*: observations in and of mirrored consciousness. In this way, one comes upon limit-observations that cannot be brought into the experiential sphere unless one energetically takes up exercises of consciousness. One can then pursue introspection on other planes.

The studies were written for readers oriented toward anthroposophical spiritual science, though much will not be incomprehensible for other, psychologically-minded readers. Readers oriented toward R. Steiner's work will naturally pose the question: to what extent is this to be found in Steiner? A twofold meaning is hidden in this question. In presentations based on spiritual investigation, one always finds only what one is in a position to find–either before the act of reading or from the act of reading, which act must be, or should be, meditative. In this sense, then, the answer to the question's second meaning could be: everything presented here is to be found in Steiner's works, though often only in hints and aphorisms. Nor did he work on the questions treated here as comprehensively as, for example, he described the problem of human freedom.

A few comments on the question of terminology are called for. The most difficult riddle for a reader of Steiner's psychological discussions and comments may be that he generally makes no distinction between the terms "supraconscious," "subconscious," "unconscious," but uses these expressions interchangeably and irregularly, just as elsewhere he has no completely fixed terminology. We can assume that this occurs for pedagogical reasons: we are not meant to understand these words nominalistically. And we should also realize that in his day the technical language of psychology was not as well known or as commonly used as today.

For this reason it is not surprising, though it is regrettable, that psychologically interested readers and even authors have overlooked the few passages in which Steiner clearly and explicitly distinguishes between supra- and subconscious, and have passed over the many passages in which the distinction is there in meaning, but without these two terms. Hence a considerable confusion arose with regard to the "subconscious" of analytic psychology and its relation to Steiner's presentation. I have tried to clear up these misunderstandings in Chapter 3 and to present new conclusions. Chapter 2 is an attempt to describe cognitive life from a viewpoint outside the plane of everyday consciousness.

Chapter 4 is certainly the most difficult to understand. Therein lies another terminological question. R. Steiner hardly distinguishes between the various types of memory and generally treats the complex of related questions from very different viewpoints; generally, it is not memory that stands at the center of the description, but, for example, the activity of the etheric body, the astral body, etc.

This brings us to the next terminological problem. Steiner only distinguishes explicitly between the etheric body and the free etheric energies when he is specifically concerned with making this distinction. It is the same with the astral body and its free energies. Whoever pursues questions systematically in Steiner's work will find this distinction to be very important on the one hand, while discovering, on the other, that its sense can be found in the texts.

Finally, there remains the question of why in these essays I for the most part avoid the expressions "etheric" and "astral" and replace them with others. It is not because these expressions have been freighted with excess meaning by spiritistic and other nebulous forms of occultism. Above all, I wanted to prevent the reader's being spared the effort of forming concepts anew, to prevent his meeting familiar "technical terms" with representations after the manner of mirrored consciousness rather than with concepts of a higher order.

For the initial impulse to regard the life of the soul on a spiritual-scientific basis, I am indebted to Massimo Scaligero's *Psicoterapia* (Roma, 1974). Though my formulation contradicts this work in many points, I want to express my gratitude for the stimulation it provided.

I am aware that the presentation of individual questions is neither complete nor error-free: infallibility is a very rare human quality. I would be happy if these attempts stimulated professionals to further thoughts on this theme–to supplement them, even to correct them.

Becoming Aware of the Logos

The Way of St. John the Evangelist

Georg Kühlewind

A single human being has no reality; the existence of "man" begins with the word that floats between me and you. The logos connects human beings through the Word; all else is temptation or a temporary connection.

The fruit of many years of study and meditation, *Becoming Aware of the Logos* places the reader in the world of living thinking and cognitive love. It teaches the way of grace and truth in a radical, original manner. For the logos, although it is the ground of any true logic, is beyond ordinary dialectic. The author does not approach his subject conventionally, but penetrates and communicates it through the unfolding of central themes such as: the logos as speech and relationship; the logos in the beginning; the light in the darkness; the speaker; life; spirit; grace and truth.

196 pp   ISBN 0-940262-09-6

From Normal to Healthy

Paths to the Liberation of Consciousness

Georg Kühlewind

How much practical time do we usually devote to the general art of being human? This guide to the self-healing of consciousness–it is both a spiritual psychology and a contemporary manual of the inner life–begins by laying out very clearly the unhealthy, unfree nature of today's "normal" consciousness. Methodical, phenomenological self-observation leads to the discovery of the key to the liberation of consciousness from its habitual blinkers and automatisms: the realization of the universal primacy of cognition and the universal availability of its ground, the free attention.

By the use of these faculties, a person, practicing the exercises given by the author, begins to expand the range of his or her possibilities of understanding and doing. The exercises–based upon the Eightfold Path of the Buddha and the cognitive path of Rudolf Steiner–lead to a new life in which supraconscious intuitions gradually take the place of subconscious formations. This new life is a universal-human life of improvisatory, living thinking: a life of presence, pure joy, which is health for human beings.

232 pp   ISBN 0-940262-10-X

Stages of Consciousness

Meditations on the Boundaries of the Soul

Georg Kühlewind

"To overcome the world means to behold the world as it was before it became dead in us; to behold it in its aliveness, as heaven. To overcome the world means to behold the earth in the heavens and to bring the heavens to earth."

Ordinarily we live under the tyranny of the past. All that we call thinking is the habitual association of finished, dead thoughts. But these thoughts were alive once and every new moment of understanding is a breath from the level of the living present.

Stages of Consciousness proposes that we school ourselves in that stage of consciousness we occasionally glimpse as intuition.

144 pp   ISBN 0-940262-08-8

Order from: LINDISFARNE PRESS
                RR 4, BOX 94 A 1
                HUDSON, NY 12534
Telephone: 518-851-9155

If you are interested in Lindisfarne Press publications write for a complete catalog to the above address.